From Bucket List To Best Self

Shane O'Brien

*"Life is not about finding yourself;
it is about creating yourself."*

George Bernard Shaw

Dedication

TO MY CHILDREN, through this book and my actions, may you learn what I have learned. My hope is that you can be who you were supposed to be and reach heights I never could. Be your best self and may your bucket list be full of adventures.

To my wife, thank you for allowing me to be myself in a world that is constantly trying to make me something else. Thank you for your encouragement to write this book. If it wasn't for your confidence in me, I'm not sure this book would have ever materialised. The lessons I've learned would've just been kept to myself.

To Rose, thank you for your editing of this book. You brought an efficiency and comprehension to my book that I never could. Your kind words and faith allowed me to see the value in my work that my sense of inferiority would not allow, so thank you for that.

About the Author

SHANE O'BRIEN IS A PSYCHOLOGY GRADUATE, property developer, entrepreneur, and avid traveller.

"From Bucket List to Best Self" is a captivating exploration of personal growth, drawing on Shane's academic background in psychology and his diverse life experiences. Through a blend of research, personal anecdotes, and travel adventures, Shane offers readers a fresh and inspiring take on how to transform their lives and achieve their full potential.

Shane's ability to seamlessly weave together his academic knowledge with real-world experiences sets "From Bucket List to Best Self" apart as a truly unique and valuable contribution to the self-help genre. His passion for personal development and his engaging writing style makes this book a must-read for anyone seeking to embark on a journey of self-discovery and growth.

Table of Contents

CHAPTER ONE

Age is just a number

WHEN I SET OUT TO WRITE THIS BOOK, I had the title: "Bucket list before Thirty" in mind. However, I realised that would convey the wrong message. It would suggest that a bucket list should only be tackled when you're young and carefree. That's an absolute lie. Age has no relevance in this book, except for the fact that I personally completed my original bucket list before the age of thirty. Notice, I completed my 'original' bucket list before the age of thirty. The moment I completed it; I made a new bucket list.

Why?

Happiness, fulfilment and contentment are not a destination, they're a journey. I conquered some fears, gained self-confidence and learned to rely on myself. I discovered how to accept adversity and overcome it. I travelled the world and had some amazing times, but…

There's always more to see, more to experience and more room to develop.

I'm not restricted by disease or sickness (fortunately). I haven't reached a state of enlightenment or self-actualisation (yet). In fact, I'm far from it. Why would I stop challenging myself to be a better person and enjoying my life? I may not travel as vigorously as before, but I spend a lot of time implementing the knowledge that I gained from travelling into my everyday life.

The bucket list is a pivotal part of my life and it will be until the day I die. However, when I started, it was more about destinations, experiences and a journey of self-understanding. Now, I know more about who I am and what I value. I have met people from other countries who value different things. As a result, I don't feel the need to conform to my culture. I've created a life that mirrors my own values; not those of society. I know I'm still learning about myself and will do until the day I die.

I've learned that I'm not the sum of my successes or failures; I am the process of their attainment. I am the most in tune with myself when I'm in the midst of my bucket list. I am a man with a plan; the intent to learn and achieve.

A bucket list provides you with a goal and a direction. Your life can be changed by the process of attaining the goals on your list.

I am not some hot-shot world adventurer who has travelled to over forty countries. I am a person who knows what he enjoys. I am not an influencer who takes photos for Instagram, but someone who wants to look back on his memories when he's old and grey.

Your bucket list should be looked at the same way: it's not about focusing on the end goal, but enjoying the personal journey.

The bucket list never ends.

It doesn't matter when you start, only that you have started it; and that you're fully intentional about your personal journey.

CHAPTER TWO

What is a Bucket List?

A BUCKET LIST WILL GIVE YOU intentionality, purpose and direction. It will bring you self-awareness and accountability for your life. A list will help you to devise a plan; not just of places to see, but also experiences that will help you grow and develop. If done correctly, a bucket list reveals your unmet desires, insecurities and passions.

A bucket list must be embarked upon despite lurking fears or anxieties. Recognising its power over us, we can have the desire to understand fear and surpass it. The process of challenging fear, both physically and emotionally, will make you a better person. It will force you to reach your potential whilst providing you with fulfilment, self-confidence and memories to last a lifetime. A bucket list allows you to develop emotionally at your own pace. It gives you a sense of control amidst a chaotic world by forcing you to focus on the end goal.

It will inspire you to create and tackle goals you want to achieve before you leave this world. By having a bucket list, you become intentional with your life. As such, you attack life and seize the day.

A bucket list gives your life a goal; a goal to live life to YOUR fullest and be the best you can be. The positive effect of having a bucket list is best summarised by Walt Whitman:

> *"Keep your face toward the sun and the shadows will fall behind you."*

By having a bucket list, you are positioning yourself towards the sun. You are giving your life direction and purpose in the form of personal growth and self-discovery. This focus on personal growth will allow you to let other, less unimportant, aspects of life fade away; such as the rat race, material possessions or your social standing in society.

Now you have an idea of what a bucket list can do for you. But first, what exactly is a bucket list?

The Oxford dictionary describes a bucket list as "a number of experiences or achievements that a person hopes to have, or accomplish, during their lifetime."

The term 'bucket list' became mainstream when it was coined by screenwriter Justin Zackham in his screenplay for the 2007 film 'The Bucket List'. The origin of the term 'bucket list' is derived from a list of experiences to do before you 'kick the bucket' (in other words, before you die). The list is not just a set of destinations, but also a list of achievements or experiences. The experience must be valued over the destination.

Take the example of travelling to Paris. Let's say you go to Paris for a few hours, spot the Eiffel Tower from a distance, then get a flight home. You have effectively completed the bucket list task of: "seeing the Eiffel tower in Paris".

However, let's say you've always wanted to go to France. It would be a much more intrinsically rewarding experience if you experience a new culture, try 'Escargots de Bourgogne' (snails baked in their shells), visit the Eiffel tower, take some time to walk around and sense the atmosphere.

The first scenario involves checking a task off a list, using minimal effort. The second scenario however, involves immersing oneself in an experience that will fundamentally improve one's outlook. Not only have you made time to do something they've always wanted to do, but you've left your comfort zone to do so. When we achieve something we've always wanted to do, it boosts our self-esteem and improves our outlook on life.

Don't get me wrong, there's nothing wrong with grabbing an opportunity for a quick trip. In fact, I'd encourage it. It's better to experience a small taster of something, than never to taste it at all. However, a bucket list should be approached with a view to experiencing the ideal scenario in its fullest, rather than just ticking it off a list.

Some experiences may not be what you thought they'd be. Of course, it's still okay to tick them off the list. As long as you were open-minded to the experience, regardless of the outcome, you will have learned from it. Not all your bucket list Items will be completed in a well-planned, well-scheduled manner. Some will be completed simply by taking advantage of an opportunity that has presented itself. This can often be the most rewarding as there's no time to overthink it.

These spontaneous opportunities usually arise after you've tackled a few items on your list. You've witnessed the joy and personal growth it brought you. As a result, you're open to experiences and able to seize the opportunities life throws your way.

Create a bucket list, not out of obligation, but for emotional growth and development. One of the few negatives anyone can say about making a bucket list is that you risk spending precious time and money visiting destinations you feel obligated to see. Perhaps some people feel driven by superficial reasons such as trying to convey a lifestyle or portray a certain image that they don't really feel. You should travel to places and create experiences that you want to do, simply for you and nobody else. Only when you do this, will you develop and grow throughout the highs and lows of a bucket list. We will look at this in greater detail later when we examine my bucket list and discuss how to create your own list.

"Travel is an investment in yourself."

– The Cultureur

It is not an investment for others.

If it's not written, it's not going to happen

I completed my bucket list by the age of 30. How?

I had written it down on a piece of paper, therefore I had a physical list to look at. The list was sellotaped to my bedroom wall where I could see it every day. When I moved house, the list moved house. When I wanted to edit my list, I rewrote it and stuck a new piece of paper up. There was always something tangible to focus on. It might not have coordinated with my partner's interior decorating, but it stayed nonetheless.

Having a list that I could see on a daily basis made me accountable. When I completed a task, there was a sense of satisfaction when I got to tick it off my list. Every time I walked past my list and saw a task ticked off, it gave me a lift.

In addition, having my list written down made my goals feel real and concrete. My aspirations were no longer abstract thoughts in my head. My thoughts were words on a page, as real as you and me.

The strategy of writing down your goals is supported by numerous studies. Findings show that outlining your goals in writing makes you far more likely to succeed.

> *"People who write down and visualise their goals are up to 1.4 times more likely to successfully accomplish them."*

> *(Murphy, 2017)*

There's a huge difference between simply writing down your goals and visualising them. There are good reasons as to why this is the case.

Firstly, from a biological perspective, information is more memorable through 'encoding'. Encoding is the process by which the things we visualise in our minds become transformed into memories.

By writing down our goals, we are forcing our brains to see the goal in our mind. These images travel to the hippocampus where they're analysed. From there, decisions are made about what is thrown away and what is stored in our long-term memory. Writing down our goal improves the chances it will be encoded and stored in our long-term memory.

In layman's terms, when you write down your goal, it has a much greater chance of being remembered.

Neuropsychologists have also found that information is remembered if it's generated from your own mind rather than being simply heard or read. Your brain will remember something far better when you create it in your own mind. Parents of small kids will see this in action when they're creating and playing with imaginary friends.

This is called 'The Generation Effect'. By writing down a goal, you get to initiate the generation effect twice:

1. First by thinking of it.
2. Second, by thinking of it again when you write it down.

Your bucket list must be physically written (or typed) and displayed somewhere that it can be seen regularly.

Write it down to keep it right

When most people think about the term 'bucket list', they usually imagine visiting destinations such as Paris, Milan or Istanbul. They rarely think about their personal development; what they'll learn about themselves and about the amazing people they'll meet along the way. Yes, seeing the sights is important. The feeling you get when you've finally visited the sights you've always wanted to see is extremely important for personal satisfaction and contentment.

However, there's a massive downfall to only focusing on extrinsic places and not on intrinsic development. If you focus solely on sights, experiences and extrinsic factors, you'll always want more and never feel satisfied. It would be like drinking sea water to quench your thirst.

Perhaps you visit the most well-known places such as the Pyramids of Egypt, the Empire State Building and Colosseum of Rome. You talk to other people about their travels and discover that they too, have visited those places. You'll then feel like you have to see more.

Once you've seen the most well-known places, you'll feel like an experienced traveller. After that, you may feel the urge to discover lesser-known places and remote locations. That's okay if you're doing it for your own personal develop-ment and not just for Instagram likes!

It can be never-ending and can go on and on. Let's be honest, you could travel every day of your life and still not see a fraction of the world. That doesn't mean that we should stop trying. It just means you shouldn't send yourself on a fool's errand. It's better to structure plans in a way that benefits you.

I fell victim to this. I started travelling and loved it. I met fellow travellers who were older than me and had seen more. I felt like I had to compete. I realised I was travelling for the wrong reasons; for the approval and respect of others rather than my own self approval and self-respect.

I had a moment of clarity in Podgorica, Montene-gro. I met a guy who had been travelling continuously for two years. In awe, I asked him how he afforded it. He told me that he wrote reviews and tips for a blog and travel magazine. He could decide where he wanted to travel except for occasions when he was sent to certain coun-tries due to a particular demand.

It sounded like my dream job.

In my eyes, he was so lucky. Life was an adven-ture every day. He had no responsibilities and no cares. He travelled solo. He was single and open to romances along the way. *How great this life must be!* I thought. I was so jealous!

I spent three days in Podgorica and chatted to him whenever the opportunity arose. He was ten years older than me. The more I talked to him, the more I learned about his life back home. He had fallen out with his parents. His relationship had ended. A lot of his friends had settled down and didn't seem to have time for him anymore, especially the ones with kids. He seemed tired of travelling as most of his time was spent in the hostel.

He lacked my own new-found enthusiasm. I was getting to see a select number of sights on my time-limited trip. Unfortunately, my new acquaintance seemed lonely. His adventure and excitement of travelling was used to disguise the fact that he was avoiding his life back home. He didn't want to see his parents and endure their judgemental attitude. He didn't want to return to a life of being single with no friends. A veil of adventure was disguising his avoidance.

Since spotting this behaviour, I started to notice more and more travellers who were doing the same. It is one of the downfalls to travelling and sightseeing; it can be used for avoidance and stagnation. As human beings, we all need some adventure in our life. The amount of adventure varies from one person to the next but we all need some change in our lives from time to time. It is one of the many reasons why prison is awful. It's monotonous; the same cell and the same inmates day in, day out.

We need variety in our lives and a sense of adventure, at least to some degree.

However, adventure on its own can also fall into that same familiarity. Whatever we experience often enough starts to diminish our responses. Even after travelling for a long period of time, we become desensitised to its pleasure.

It's important not to use travelling as a means of avoiding problems. If you do so, the cure becomes your poison. There's an old Irish saying: *"A rolling stone gathers no moss"*, which means that people need consistency and routine to grow. If you're moving from place to place, it's hard to develop meaningful relationships or thrive in a career.

Travelling should be used as a means to develop our life and add to it, not as our sole focus.

If / when creating the travel part of your bucket list, make sure to write your preferred destinations down. That way, you won't be tempted to add extras, having been influenced by a new travel trend.

Once the list is written, you'll have a stable target. Once completed, it will give you satisfaction and a sense of accomplishment. It will also prevent you from moving the goalposts.

The aim of writing it down is to start the process and give you intentionality. It is best described by Mark Victor Hansen:

> *"By recording your dreams and goals on paper, you set in motion the process of becoming the person you most want to be."*

Set your dreams in motion and write a list!

Intentionality

Creating a bucket list gave me a massive sense of direction, intentionality and purpose. Even though I was quite young when I created my first bucket list, it gave me a real sense of urgency. When I had free time, I could look at the next goal on my list, research how to do it and set a date to put it in motion.

One of my goals was to see a number of Irish sights. When I was bored or had no weekend plans, I'd set off in my car and visit one of the sights. If I didn't have a list, I wouldn't have been so intentional with my time. I would have just watched TV or gone drinking like any other young lad.

If several weeks passed and I hadn't tackled anything on my list, I would look at it and feel bad. Realising that I was wasting my time, it would spur me on to tackle another task or see another sight. The list gave me a sense of urgency and a sense of accountability. No one else was going to help me complete the list. Why would they? It was my list. I had to do it for myself.

Intentionality is the most significant gift a bucket list gives you.

You watch a movie based in a country you'd like to visit, you read a travel magazine full of destinations you'd love to see, your parents tell you stories about fantastic places they visited. So, what do you do? You do absolutely nothing.

We always think we have all the time in the world, but we do not.

We never know when our time is up or what's around the corner. It's tempting to fall into the trap of thinking that we're only young and we'll get around to it eventually. And yet, the older we get, the more responsibilities we will acquire. The more responsibilities we have, the less time we'll have to do what we want to do.

By writing down your bucket list and displaying it clearly where you can see it, you are starting your personal journey TODAY.

There's never a reason to start tomorrow. There's always something that can be started **right now.**

Even if bedridden in hospital, a resourceful patient could be researching the things to do after recovery.

You could practise meditation or mindfulness if that is on your list. You could apologise to someone for something you feel guilty for.

There's so much you can do right now, but only when you're intentional with your time.

Grouping tasks or destinations together

Writing my bucket list down on paper helped me, not only to set my intentions, but also to make a concrete plan to achieve my goals. The physical bucket list helped me prioritise and group together certain tasks that could be completed around the same time. Bearing in mind, I started my bucket list at the age of twenty. I prioritised tasks that I could do as a young adult with no kids, as opposed to later down the line when there could be young kids and big responsibility.

For example, I wanted to travel by train through Europe. That was a priority as it was possible sooner rather than later. I wanted to travel to Scandinavia, however the cost of living is pretty high in countries such as Norway, Sweden and

Denmark. These countries were too expensive for a college kid like me, so I placed them further down the list. They could be tackled when I was older, when I'd be earning a salary after college.

However, one of my friends was studying abroad in Denmark so I was able to visit her for a week. I got to see Denmark and I had my own personal tour guide! Thanks to my friend, I was getting accommodation for the price of a few drinks on a night out.

Some of my goals overlapped. For example, I wanted to travel on a 'J1' which is a 3-month working Visa in the United States. I also wanted to go to Vegas, drink lots and have a great time. So, I strategically chose to do a J1 in California within driving distance of Vegas.

When planning the execution of your goals, try to group the ones that can be done in unison in one trip. This will maximise your efficiency and shave some time off your bucket list. It also prevents you from procrastinating about certain nerve-wrecking tasks.

For example, I was nervous about going scuba diving. I've had a fear of the water ever since I was a young child and I tragically found out my best friend had drowned. However, I was invited to a wedding in Croatia so I grouped together as many sights and goals that I could complete on that trip. I was certainly not ready for scuba diving! I panicked several times during the session and had to resurface. That experience motivated me to sign up for swimming lessons when I returned home. I wanted to feel more secure in the water and I would never have taken that positive step if I hadn't pushed myself to go scuba diving. I'm happy to say that I was able to try scuba diving again several years later and I enjoyed it much more that time.

The moral of the story though, is that by grouping tasks together, I couldn't avoid any challenging quests. I was forced to take action and tackle it.

Don't put off until tomorrow something you could do today!

As well as grouping goals together, I mentioned earlier that you will have to make the most of any opportunity that comes your way. These opportunities present themselves all the time but we rarely avail of them.

Let's say a friend moves to New Zealand. We wave goodbye, promising we'll be over to visit them and picturing an idyllic trip with an old friend. Two years pass by and they return home. They bump into us in the same pub we've been going to every weekend. They ask us why we never came out to visit them in New Zealand. We spend several hours asking them all about their trip and telling them it's "on the bucket list".

I get it—we can't just quit our jobs and clear off to New Zealand, but we could have prioritised going there for a vacation, especially as a friend was offering free accommodation!

In my experience, opportunities always present themselves.

> *"Opportunities multiply once seized."*
>
> – *Sun Tza*

You could travel somewhere, then meet a friend of a friend. This person is from a country you've always wanted to visit. You get chatting and hit it off. They give you great advice about the sights, telling you about all the hidden gems to see in their country. Then, boom! They invite you to come stay with them when they return next year.

This happens all the time. Perhaps you'd rather stay in your own accommodation, however you've just collected great advice about a country you haven't yet researched. Even if you don't stay with them, you might meet up with them for a night while they show you around their city. It will most likely enhance your experience of their city, not to mention reinstate your faith in humanity!

My friend's cousin had come over from Canada with her friends. I had planned to go to Canada later that year with the Erasmus exchange programme. Although I felt too shy to talk to her, I summoned up the courage and called her over. It turned out that she lived an hour from the University I'd be going to. Her family collected me from the airport and dropped me to my college apartment. They even gave me all their daughter's old college supplies such as plates, cutlery and a microwave. They saved me hundreds of dollars and showed me how kind humans can be. It really did reinstate my faith in humanity. This all happened because I availed of an opportunity that presented itself. Sometimes it will be more difficult than others. You might not even get any return. However, some of the best experiences come from seizing opportunities.

During my travels, I had several experiences where I received true kindness from people. In Montenegro, my girlfriend and I travelled from the capital Podgorica to Ostrog monastery. Ostrog Monastery is situated against an almost vertical background, high up in the large mountain rock of Ostroška Greda. It is dedicated to Saint Basil of Ostrog, who was buried there. The bus dropped us off at the side of the motorway and we had to walk several miles to get to the top of the mountain. A man, in the most beat-up car I had ever seen, stopped and gestured that he'd give us a lift. Reluctantly, we got in. He drove us to the top of the mountain, navigating dangerous bends. All the while, we had clear views straight to the bottom. Our hearts were in our mouths the whole time. He tried to make small talk but we spoke different languages. It was more like a game of charades. He eventually dropped us off, saving us two or three hours of walking. He refused to take a five euro note for the lift. Then he refused a two-euro coin. He even refused a one-euro coin. When I tried to leave the two euros in the car, he picked it up, walked after me and handed it back. Going by the appearance of his car, he could have done with the money, but he wanted to do a kind act for someone. To this day, I still remember it. I can't remember all the destinations I've been to, but I can remember all the times I was shown true kindness.

What is luck?

Opportunities have come my way and friends often comment "You're so lucky". Also, people have looked at my social media and remark: "You're so lucky to have been where you've been and seen what you've seen."

Am I lucky though?

Luck is defined as "success brought on by chance rather than one's own actions or intentions". Am I lucky to have made a strategic list of goals and destinations, then prioritised them in such a way to integrate them into my life?

Am I lucky that I worked, saved and budgeted for them?

If that is luck, then it's a lot harder than I thought. I know I wasn't lucky but I was prepared, consistent and dedicated. I just agree with them and reply that yes, I am lucky. Then I add a quote by Seneca:

> *"Luck is what happens when opportunity meets preparedness."*

At this point, they just nod in agreement, even though I know they have no idea what I mean. If they questioned me further, I would tell them that my travels are only the result of creating a bucket list. By having a list, you are prepared. The only way I feel lucky is that I gained the perspective to write a list. I then used it to challenge myself, which brought me joy and helped me to develop as a person.

Not everyone writes a bucket list. Even fewer write a bucket list with the goal of personal development and challenging themselves. As a result, few people experience the intrinsic value which comes from a bucket list. This, in turn, reduces their motivation to complete their list. Based on my experience, I'll tell you what the average person does in relation to setting out goals in order to promote self-development in their life.

They do nothing!

Most people don't write a bucket list. Instead, they wander aimlessly through life. They take holidays based on recommendations from friends or via their Instagram feed. By booking package holidays which require no planning, they end up with hugely overpriced deals.

For the small few that do write a list, they collate a number of abstract destinations with only a few goals they're sure they can complete. Most destinations will mirror the superficial and commercial values of society with little to no individuality. They write down a number of places which resembles something from a Top Ten Google search; The Grand Canyon, The Colosseum and the Sydney Opera house. These are amazing places and are definitely worth a visit, but there's no individuality in their choices.

To be honest, most people don't have a clue what they want or who their authentic self is. They've never even thought about it. I asked one guy what was on his bucket list. He said: "Nothing! I'm not dying!" He thought bucket lists were only for people who were terminally ill. Bucket lists are not for people who are dying; they are for people who truly want to live. They are for people who want to experience this world, seeing what they've always wanted to see, and becoming the person they've always wanted to be.

I've asked a lot of people about their bucket list. The most common response is: "I haven't thought about it." Most people have no intentions for what they want to achieve in life. Life just happens to them. They often end up in destinations that are popular on social media; places they think will increase their social acceptability. The problem is that some people lack intentionality, or they lack the self-awareness to be intentional. People aren't aware of their hidden values and strengths; of what truly makes them happy. Before you write your bucket list, it's important to become self-aware first, which we'll discuss in greater detail later in this book.

Desire

There's a common misconception before creating a bucket list. Some people think that once you've written a list, it will all just happen effortlessly. They believe that achieving goals, seeing amazing destinations and having great experiences will just magically happen as a result of writing a list. They think that simply creating a goal is all they have to do.

I can say, with utmost confidence, this is not the case.

Anything that is worth achieving takes a huge amount of desire and some form of suffering. Goals aren't achieved without applying yourself consistently.

When I was in my final year of primary school, at twelve years of age, I had a teacher; let's call him Freddie. Freddie was a strong man and an inspired character who demanded respect and, if I'm honest, instilled a bit of fear amongst his students. He was an educator by trade but to me, teaching was his calling. He educated us in more than just academia; he also taught morals, principles and character virtues. He did this for decades despite having his own personal demons. Most people have a handful of people who really shape their lives and I had the pleasure of being a student of Freddie. Amid his school lessons, he also sprinkled quality life advice. At the time, it seemed to wash over me, but years later, his pearls of wisdom came back to me.

One of my friends didn't really apply himself at school and one day, he hadn't completed his homework. Freddie, who was appalled by this, cited a quote from Erma Bomebeck:

> *"When I stand before God at the end of my life,*
> *I would hope that I would not have a single bit*

*of talent left, and could say, 'I used everything
you gave me and I have nothing left.'"*

He asked my friend: "What would you say to
God or Saint Peter at the gates of heaven? How
would you explain why you should get in? How
would you justify what you'd done with your
life?"

Freddie went on to encourage my friend by
pointing out all his talents; assets that he wasn't
utilising to his full capacity.

This conversation stuck with me, not because of
religious views, but it made me think about
having to justify my life. It was a concept that, at
the age of twelve, I hadn't thought about. Perhaps
it's a concept that very few people think about.
However, I vowed to myself, there and then, that
I would apply myself in whatever I would do. I
would stand before God and report that I had
used my talents and didn't waste my life.

As I grew into adulthood, my mind changed over
time. Experiences I'd had, books I'd read and key
people who shaped my life had altered my
perceptions. Today, I believe it's not about
standing before God but rather, standing before
ourselves. Can we say that we've used our talents
to the best of our ability and applied ourselves in
all that we did?

Some people don't apply themselves at all. Some people only partly apply themselves. Some apply themselves in particular areas of their lives: their job, their education or their family. However, most people don't apply themselves fully in all aspects of their life. Fewer still apply themselves with regard to their personal development. For most, it's not even a thought.

Embarking on a bucket list with a view to improving your personal development is absolutely pointless if you don't have the desire. You need to tap into your inner child's desire to be the best you can be and reach your potential. I think most people gain motivation when they think of the end goal. So, as morbid as it sounds, imagine yourself on your deathbed, having to justify your life. Whether it's to God, St Peter, the grim reaper, whatever helps you visualise. Let that conversation steer your life. Think about using your gifts to the fullest potential instead of just existing through life. If you do this, you honestly can't go wrong.

Wrong reasons

Before we get into the nitty-gritty of how and why to make a bucket list, there is one thing I must be adamant about: making a bucket list is not a race. It's not a contest with your neighbours, friends or family! It's not about the latest societal trend, showing off or making yourself out to be something you're not.

Your desire to be the best you can be shouldn't result in others feeling bad about themselves. Sharing photos of your adventures on social media isn't a bad thing. However, it is toxic behaviour if you end up thinking you're better than someone that hasn't travelled.

Don't rub your experiences in someone else's face. Don't gloat to someone who may not have had the same opportunities you've had.

Travelling shouldn't be a way of 'keeping up with the Jones'. Your reasons for travelling shouldn't be just so you can be like your friends. You certainly shouldn't travel to please others. If this is the situation, then you're living someone else's life and not your own.

It's also not a way of making up for your shortcomings. A change in circumstances doesn't fix a defect of character. If you're not happy with who you are and want to escape for a while, you'll still be the same person when you return. So, to tackle this, it's important to focus on the personal development side of the bucket list, not just the sightseeing.

Finally, a common theme among travellers is that they use a bucket list as a means of avoidance, which I've touched on earlier. I've met people who talk about how much they love travelling, but then proceed to tell me how much they hated life at home and don't want to return. Unfortunately, a "rolling stone gathers no moss." This is an old proverb which means that if you're constantly moving, it's hard to grow roots, build meaningful friendships or have a thriving relationship with a partner. The point I'm trying to make is, this process should bring intrinsic value to your life; joy, happiness and a sense of accomplishment. However, it shouldn't be used to avoid negative emotions such as fear, judgement or loss. In addition, if you're embarking upon a bucket list to feel like you're someone of worth, then you might feel great for about two weeks after it's complete. Then you'll go back to feeling empty.

Use the process of doing a bucket list to help you work on aspects of yourself that you don't like. Alternatively, you can use it to push yourself out of your comfort zone. For example, you might realise that you're co-dependent in a relationship and feel as though you're not capable of dealing with life on your own. If the relationship ends, it may be the perfect time to go solo travelling for a week. You'll realise that actually, you're very competent. You must lean into fear, in order to grow.

However, if you're doing a bucket list to try to be someone you're not, then you'll end up chasing one adventure after the other. You may even put yourself under financial pressure in order to book that next flight, just so you can feel adventurous again. It's no joke, it can be as addictive as alcohol or drugs. So, travel for the right reasons and make sure the bucket list is in line with your own values. We will discuss values in greater detail later in this book).

Disclaimer

Before we continue, I want to provide you with a disclaimer of sorts:

I am no guru.

I am not a professional traveller and I'm certainly not an influencer on social media. I'm not a YouTuber and I'm not well-known outside my local area. In my eyes, I'm not even a writer! I am borderline dyslexic and I have dysgraphia which means I struggle with grammar. To be honest, English was never my best subject. You better believe that this book was proofread and edited by many people, all of whom are better at conveying thoughts and emotions than me. People who studied hard in school and got an A in English. However, despite knowing what I'm not, I also know what I am.

I am not ordinary. That doesn't mean I have superpowers or some grandiose sense of self-worth bordering on narcissism. I am not ordinary because I do not think ordinarily.

If I'm not already happy, I don't believe that becoming wealthy will make me happy. If one of my posts gets lots of 'likes', I don't think that will somehow give me status. I don't believe that life is long enough to wander around aimlessly without having a goal, direction or purpose.

The fact is, the only thing that differentiates me to most people, is that I have a different perspective on life. I value my life so much that I feel I need to have a purpose and direction. Not all heroes wear capes and not all extraordinary feats are done by extraordinarily gifted people. Most extraordinary feats are achieved by ordinary people with a different perspective from the norm. They have attributes such as consistency, determination and not being afraid to go against the grain. These people are happy to be their authentic selves. These people dance like no-one is watching, just because they enjoy it. They take part in Karaoke even if their singing is terrible, but just because they enjoy it.

Essentially, they know who they are. They know what their values are and they know what they like. They are okay if people don't like them, think their dancing sucks or believe they can't hold a note in their head.

Regardless, they are content in their own skin.

I would hope that when anyone completes their bucket list, this is what they feel like:

Content in their own skin.

I hope, upon completion of your bucket list, that you're more self-aware, confident and content. Anyone who completes their bucket list is an extraordinary person. They are resilient, consistent and wise. To self-actualise, we must know ourselves and undergo a process of transformation.

This book aims to give you as much value that is needed to promote growth and self-actualisation, in as many areas of personal development as possible. However, the topics discussed hold depth and weight; they will take time to understand. Each section, such as desire, fear, etc, could have an array of books dedicated to that one topic alone.

This book aims to open your eyes to different theories and to show you how to use them practically. We want to convert theory to practical application. However, on your journey, you may need to delve deeper into certain areas. Please do.

This book will start you off and guide you on your journey of personal development. The book is not all-knowing, however knowledge is power, so please read and learn as much as you can. This book does not provide all knowledge in all areas, so if there are certain areas you're struggling with, you may need to explore them in more detail. This book will give you an entry-level approach to personal development and how a bucket list will help you to begin your journey. However, the journey of personal development is different for everyone. This book is just an aid to your journey, not a bible. You are the master of your own life.

CHAPTER THREE

Self-actualization

BEFORE WE EMBARK ON OUR JOURNEY of devising a bucket list to become our best selves, we must set off with the end in mind. What does it mean to be our best selves? What is the state of being our best selves called? There are many names for being our best selves in many different religions. In Buddhist practice, they call the height of personal development 'reaching a state of enlightenment'. In Christianity, you may be annotated as a saint or be considered a holy person. However, for us in this book, I am going to use the scientific term of self-actualization. The term 'self-actualization' was first used by American psychologist Abraham Maslow. Self-actualisation is the highest level of psychological development, where "actualization" is the fulfilment of one's talents and potentialities. Self-actualization is reaching one's potential in all aspects of one's life; emotionally, spiritually and financially. It is based on the premise that everyone has a driving desire to reach their own potential. These human needs were created by American psychologist Abraham Maslow. They are called *Maslow's hierarchy of needs*. Maslow made a table conveying all the various needs that motivate human behaviour. The table is displayed as a pyramid, with the lowest levels representing basic needs and more complex needs located at the top of the pyramid.

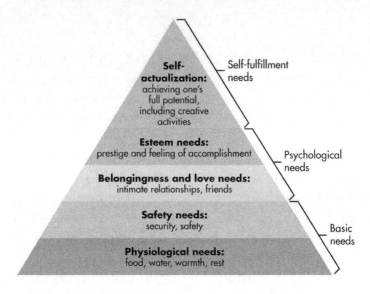

The first four levels are often referred to as 'deficiency needs'; if unmet, they could cause physical and psychological discomfort. The motivation to fulfil these needs grows the longer we are deprived of them. For example, on a physical level, the longer one goes without food, the hungrier one becomes. Psychologically, the longer a person is deprived of intimacy and affection, the more they will try to fill that void. Maslow states that individuals must satisfy lower-level needs before moving up to the next need. However, it is not an all-or-nothing phe-nomenon; you can still move up to the next level if a need is not 100% addressed. Therefore, those of us with scars, who need more time to fulfil deficiency needs, can still thrive and develop at other levels. We are not stagnant by any means.

The fifth level is self-fulfilling and is a growth need. Growth needs are not motivated by deprivation but by desire; a desire to be the best you can be and a desire for personal growth. In theory, once these growth needs have been met, one should be able to reach the highest form of personal development; *self-actualization.* Every person has the capability to reach self-actualization. Unfortunately, few do, due to the immense principles required: persistence, self-awareness, authenticity and resistance to con-formity. It is a monumental task. People never set it as a goal. Moreover, it's too difficult to arrive at self-actualization by mistake. In addition, it can resemble a game of 'Snakes and Ladders'. Once you reach a certain stage, it doesn't mean you'll never fall back down a level. For example, you could have reached feelings of love and belong-ing, but then you get a divorce and your kids move out. That level of love and belonging has gone and there's a desire to fulfil that need again. Each stage is not always consistent. However, once you have satisfied a desire once, it's never as hard to satisfy it again. You never start from scratch; you will only be starting from the beginning with experience. Let's look at each individual stage.

1. **Physiological needs**—these are biological requirements for human survival, e.g., oxygen, nutrition, water, shelter, clothing and sleep.

If these needs are unmet, the person will most likely die. Maslow considered physiological needs the most important as all the other needs become secondary until these needs are met.

2. **Safety needs**—Once an individual's physiological needs are met, there's a need for security and safety to be fulfilled. People need some degree of certainty in their lives. They want some order in society and some control in their lives. These needs can be fulfilled by family and society.

3. **Love and belonging needs**—after physiological and safety needs have been fulfilled, the third level of human need is social and involves feelings of belonging. The need for interpersonal relationships motivates behaviour at this level.

Examples include relationships such as friendships and intimate relationships; relationships that can harbour trust, intimacy and acceptance.

4. **Self-Esteem needs** are the fourth level which Maslow classified into two categories: one is self-

esteem for oneself and the second is a desire for reputation or respect from others.

5. **Self-actualization** is the fifth and final stage. It is the highest level of psychological development where the person reaches the highest level of self-achievement. A self-actualised person has reached their full potential in all aspects of life.

You might be thinking: 'What if I don't want to be a monk, renounce all my material positions and live a life of celibacy to reach a state of self-actualisation?'

Well, the good news is, you don't have to!

The bucket list is a journey and Maslow's hierarchy of needs is a guidepost. It will help you to see the aspects you might lack in your personal development. When you discover the areas in which you are lacking, you can add them to your list.

I lacked self-confidence and self-esteem. It undermined my ability to be fully independent.

What did I do to conquer this?

I went travelling on my own for two weeks!

After that experience, I know I can rely on myself. I'm not afraid to be alone with my thoughts.

Let's say you feel lacking when it comes to communication with others. Perhaps one of the goals on your list is to have open conversations with your partner so you can feel more connection and love. Or perhaps your goal is to have a conversation with your parents to have some closure about your childhood.

These goals are just as important (or maybe even more so) than the goals of sight-seeing popular spots like the Taj Mahal. Deep and meaningful conversations have as much relevance on your bucket list than sights.

Growing up, I had a friend who was older than me and sadly, suffered from manic depression. We were very close but, like all friends, we argued and had tiffs. I look back at those times and think: 'I don't know how someone wasn't killed or the police weren't called!'

The problem was, as his younger friend and close comparison, my achievements were seen as a threat to his self-worth and, as a result, his mental state. There were times when my friend would say: "It's easy for Shane." It wasn't, but that's what he believed at the time.

My friend and I were trying out for our county under-18 hurling team. He was 17 and I was 16. If I didn't make it, I'd have to wait until the following year to try again. My friend was a better hurler than me but I had performed better at the trials. I marked a talented young hurler with a big name and good reputation and kept him scoreless. My friend played well but didn't mark the same calibre of opposition I was marking. It looked like I might make the panel and my friend wouldn't. This really upset my friend's father and made him worry about his son's mental health.

For me, at the tender age of 16, it was the biggest achievement of my life. I felt resentful towards his parents for dampening my achievement. Any achievement was always associated with worry for my friend and it strained our relationship as we grew older.

It was during my psychology degree, when I discovered Maslow's hierarchy of needs, that I was finally able to process those feelings of worry and resentment.

I realised that, in order to have self-esteem, I needed to feel good about what I've achieved. To do that, I had to stop being resentful. It didn't change the past but it changed the present.

Make your personal development goals and include them on your list. Even if there's something you don't want to do immediately but you'd like to do it in the future, write it down. Someday, you may have the strength and the courage to tackle it. But if you don't write it down, you'll never make yourself accountable when the time comes.

If these personal development tasks don't scare you and challenge you, then you're only lying to yourself. This section is one of, if not the most, important section of your bucket list. Take your time and include the tasks you need to accomplish. There may only be two or three, but I assure you, that's plenty. It is this section that separates the bucket list from sights and excursions to tasks that promote personal development. These are the hardest tasks to complete, but give the highest sense of satisfaction. They really will change your life and bring you closer to self-actualization.

The characteristics of a self-actualised person and the common challenges faced in obtaining those characteristics.

I don't believe I'm a self-actualised person yet. I definitely won't be anytime soon and I may never be. I believe it is a lifelong journey. When I first heard of the term "self-actualised person," I really struggled to understand what it meant. I couldn't picture what a self-actualised person looked like. Do they have distinctive features? Can you tell if someone is self-actualised? How do self-actualised people behave? Do self-actualised people have an aura around them?

I started a journey to formulate in my mind what a self-actualised person would look like. First, I googled: "names of self-actualised people". The search brought up names such as Abraham Lincon, Albert Einstein, and the Dali Lama. These people differed so much. I wasn't sure if they had any similarities, except for the fact they had achieved great things. Some were poets, artists, scientists, politicians and spiritual leaders. At first glance, the only consistent trait seemed to be that they were old and successful. This told me that the process of self-actualisation took a long time. However, it took an even longer time for the exterior world to notice. These people had reached self-actualisation years ago, but it was only towards the end of their life that their success became renowned. How many people have self-actualised, yet we'll never know about them?

Due to the variance in occupations, I realised that occupation or calling didn't matter, the progression was internal.

Being a psychologist, I then decided to research common personality traits about self-actualised people. I was looking for consistent patterns of behaviour. I discovered articles about the characteristics of self-actualised people (Kaufman, 2018). I found six common traits:

1. Appreciation/ Gratitude

The first trait of a self-actualised person is **appreciation/gratitude**. Self-actualised people appreciate what they have, both internally and externally. They don't take their health, prosperity, friendships or loved ones for granted. A key to this is focusing on what you have, not what you don't have. We constantly compare ourselves to others as we try to fit in and stay part of the herd. Not only do we want to stay part of the herd, but we seek higher status in the herd (known as 'society'). We get upset if someone seems to be moving above us in societal status or has more material possessions. We get jealous when someone has something we want; a promotion, a bigger house, a new car, fancier clothes etc. The jealousy stems from a feeling of lack or failure. It's a double-sided coin: jealousy and failure. This can be explained by 'limited resources theory'. This theory states that someone else's success makes us feel bad about ourselves because we (our animal brains) believe there's only a certain amount of success to go around. It may have originated back to early human development. If your neighbour (or fellow tribesman) caught three fish from a small stream, you'd be worried there weren't enough fish left in the stream. There's a real threat that there may not have been.

However, for the most part, we don't struggle today for resources such as food (at least in western society). Today, it's other people's success and status that threatens us. If a neighbour (or colleague) gets the promotion or new car we crave, we feel bad about ourselves. We might even try to take that person down just to make ourselves feel better.

The farmer down the road has more cows than you.

"Oh, that's just because he has better land."

A person inherits a cafe, then expands it to make it much more profitable.

"It's easy for them—they were given a business."

We tell ourselves that if we got those chances, we could have achieved what they have achieved. We fail to take into consideration the effort, persistence and skill that person possesses to achieve such accomplishments. If tearing someone down doesn't make us feel better, then our mind turns that person into some sort of prodigy or superhuman. We make that person exceptional so that their gifts don't threaten us. By marking them as an exceptional human, we can just say: "It's easy for you, you're just an exceptionally gifted person. If I had your gifts, I would do the same."

Yet again, we dismiss the effort, sacrifice and struggle that person endured to accomplish their goals. There are many ways to avoid thinking and acting like this. One way is to develop your own sense of self-worth so that you're not threatened by others. Another way is to try not to conform to materialism or consumer society. Try to be your authentic self, which means losing the fear of other people's judgement.

These goals might seem impossible and to some, they may be. However, it's important to start being grateful for what you *do* have and start showing appreciation to those who help you. If you're grateful for what you have, you don't need to envy what others have. If you're grateful for your attributes, your meaningful relationships and your accomplishments, you'll feel fulfilled. By being grateful and appreciative, you can be happy for others without feeling jealous or like a failure. You'll save countless hours evaluating your life and comparing yourself to others.

Nowadays, most comparisons are about material possessions such as cars, houses and clothes. If you seek external factors such as wealth and possessions, you'll always want more. Craving material possessions is like drinking salt water. It gives you a moment of joy before that feeling of emptiness sets in again.

External factors are forever changing.

You might get a new job which makes you feel content. After a while, they start announcing redundancies, which triggers your fear. You might get a new car and feel wonderful taking your shiny wheels for a spin. However, months down the line, what happens if there's an unfortunate accident and the car is a write-off? You might move into a beautiful new house. As you slide your key into the lock, you might be full of pride that you're keeping up with the Joneses. However, months later, the pandemic hits. Unfortunately, that means you're out of work and you need to downsize to a smaller house.

Finances go up and they come down.

Even if you're incredibly wealthy and financially secure, your finances are probably still strongly linked to your emotions. However, they only provide momentary satisfaction.

It's more gratifying to appreciate internal successes, such as good relationships with family and friends or positive attributes such as reliability, intelligence or charisma. These attributes are constant. Appreciation and gratitude for them will keep you fulfilled and content.

This is best summarised by two quotes:

"Comparison is the thief of joy"

– Theodore Roosevelt

"Look at what you have and you will always have too much. Look at what you don't have and you will never have enough."

– Oprah Winfrey

Be grateful for what you have, start a gratitude diary and write in it each day. Make a list each day of the things you're grateful for. As you slowly start to focus on the positives in your life, this will set you on the path to self-actualisation.

2. Authenticity

The second trait of a self-actualised person is **Authenticity.** To be your authentic self is to be yourself without fear of judgement from others. Being your authentic self is behaving in a manner based on your likes, interests, principles and morality. At a very basic level, it is similar to a child before they go to school. A child is interested in whatever they like and they don't feel the need to conform to anything. They are simply happy being themself.

Being an authentic adult would mean being the same person around friends and family as you are with a board of directors in your monthly meeting. You are yourself, no matter the environment. Being authentic means being comfortable with who you are, not acting as how you think you should be.

Self-actualised, authentic people know who they are and what they like. They pursue their passions and live a life of purpose. Trying to be your authentic self can be a struggle in a world that is constantly trying to make you be something else. From a young age, we're told how to behave; that we must conform to rules to be accepted. It's important to discover who you are. In the next chapter, use the 'values exercise' to see what interests you and what changes you need to make in order to live in line with your authentic self.

3. Equanimity

Equanimity is the third characteristic that self-actualised people possess. Self-actualised people have a calmness and composure in difficult situations. They can take life's inevitable ups and downs with grace and acceptance. They develop this by accepting the things they can't change and having the courage to change the things they can. This is best conveyed by the use of the acronym *CIA (Control, Influence, Accept)*. Self-actualised people know what they can (**C**ontrol), know what they can (**I**nfluence) and they know what they must (**A**ccept).

A day-to-day example would be weight loss. You can control what you eat, you can influence your weight loss with exercise but you must accept that weight loss takes time and doesn't happen overnight.

There is a serenity in knowing what is under your control. We often worry about things we can't control, such as our children's success. Yes, we can influence their success by enrolling them in a good school and encouraging positive friendships, but we can't make decisions for them.

We worry about what the weather will be like at the weekend. We worry about the stock market or housing prices, but we don't have control over any of it. It's important to learn to control what you can, influence what you can change and accept what you can't control or influence.

Self-actualised people are immensely experienced at this and it's often this characteristic that made them famous.

The Dalai Lama was exiled from his native homeland of Tibet and took refuge in India. He controlled the situation by bringing his followers so that he could go to a safe region in India. He influenced the situation by speaking out about the Chinese government and bringing worldwide attention to the situation in Tibet. Hardest of all, he accepted what had happened and the fact that he may never return to Tibet. There will always be challenging times in everyone's life but to self-actualise, you need to learn to focus on what you can control and influence. Most of all, you need to accept the things you cannot change.

4. Purpose

Self-actualised people live a life of **purpose.** They have a great feeling of responsibility to accomplish a particular mission in their life. Having a purpose provides intentionality and resilience; strong guiding forces. We will discuss a purposeful life in detail later in this book.

5. Humanitarianism

Self-actualised people have a deep desire to help others. They send goodness out into the world without the need to get it back. Self-actualised people have heightened interpersonal relationships. They are capable of higher levels of love and fusion. They have an enhanced capability of building a connection with someone. Self-actualised people are kind and friendly, regardless of the other person's social class, education, race or nationality. The difficulty about being open to love and friendship, means that it also leaves you open to rejection, betrayal and heartache. It's very difficult to be open and convey a strong feeling of love and friendship. In order to do this, you need to develop a high sense of self-worth.

This can be done by identifying aspects of your life (both past and present) that are preventing your need for love or intimacy being met. Once identified, you can then take action to rectify this trauma through whatever means possible (e.g., counselling, a conversation with a family member, apologising for any wrongs you may have done, or just being the person you believe you should be).

Practise kindness every day. Record one act of kindness that you do each day and write it down. For example, standing up on the bus so an elderly person can take your seat. Helping a stranger on the road to change a tyre or even just holding the door open for someone. Try to do one act of kindness in conjunction with building your self-worth. Soon you'll be able to love, be a good friend and be a person that knows their worth. You'll be able to bounce back from emotional setbacks.

6. Good Moral Intuition

Good Moral Intuition is knowing what is right from wrong. You have the ability to use your own moral judgement regardless of social norms or societal influence. You can live up to your own personal morals. Self-actualised people don't allow themselves to be moulded by society. They make their own decisions, selecting what they regard as good, not just what society sees as acceptable. They don't accept societal views readily, as though they're shecp following the herd. Neither do they reject them all, like some sort of rebel. Self-actualised people have a code of ethics that is individualised and autonomous rather than being dictated by surrounding people. For example, a self-actualised person wouldn't promote or sell a product if they didn't believe it to be of value.

Lots of people sell products they secretly don't like or haven't even used. It's not illegal and it's not against societal trends, but a moral person upholds their own distinctive values. Take a look at your own life. Are you doing something that goes against your morals? If so, try to change it as soon as possible. Whatever damages your morals, also damages your soul.

These are the most common traits of a self-actualised person, briefly explained. These characteristics are the most relevant to personal growth but depending on which study you look at, there are often other characteristics.

It has to be mentioned, self-actualized people are not perfect. There are no perfect human beings. Self-actualized people are often great at personal development and have an immense emotional awareness and moral compass. They seem to be able to deflect societal influence easily but they

ARE human and are not machines. Self-actualized people have flaws; they can become tired and snap at people. They can find the weight of pressure hard to bear like the rest of us. We must give up our illusions and recognise that there are no perfect humans. There is just personal growth or stagnation. You're now on your journey of personal growth through the use of your bucket list. You are striving to be self-actualised, but most importantly you are striving for personal growth.

CHAPTER FOUR
Joy and self-actualization

WHAT SURPRISED ME THE MOST about self-actualized people was that they seemed happy in their own way, pursuing their own passions. I started to look into the characteristics of people who are happy. I reasoned that there was no point in reaching a state of self-actualization and not being happy.

What I found startling was when I read *'The Book of Joy'* by the 14th Dalai Lama, Desmond Tutu and Douglas Abrams. The book discussed the 8 pillars of Joy.

There's a big resemblance between the characteristics of a self-actualised person and the characteristics of a fulfilled, happy person. 'The Book of Joy' formulated an agreement of characteristics that people need in order to live a fulfilled, joyful life. This was observed from the two most important spiritual figures of our time, Archbishop Desmond Tutu and the Dalai Lama, who have been friends for decades. Between them, they have endured exile, violence and oppression. Yet in the face of hardships, they continued to show compassion, humour and above all, joy.

A bit of background into both spiritual leaders: Archbishop Tutu was one of South Africa's most well-known human rights activists after Nelson Mandela. He won the Nobel Peace Prize in 1984 for his efforts in ending apartheid in South Africa. Archbishop Tutu is also the first Black Anglican Archbishop of both Cape Town and Johannesburg.

The Dalai Lama is in fact the 14th in its reign. 'Dalai Lama' is the name given to the spiritual leader of Tibet. The 14th Dalai Lama assumed political power in Tibet at the age of 15. The People's Republic of China invaded that same year. Fearing violence, he (and thousands of followers) fled to Dharamshala in Northern India, where they established an alternative government. Since then, the Dalai Lama has taken numerous actions in the hopes of establishing an autonomous Tibetan state within the People's Republic of China. The Dalai Lama has also conducted hundreds of conferences, lectures and workshops worldwide. As part of his humanitarian efforts, he was awarded the Nobel Peace Prize in 1989.

Archbishop Tutu is an Anglican Christian and the Dalai Lama is a Tibetan Buddhist. However, 'The

Book of Joy' does not focus on religion. Instead, it focuses on the characteristics one needs in order to live a happy and joyful life. Despite the enormous struggles these men have faced, they have both succeeded in living joyfully.

The **8 pillars of Joy** are as follows:

1. **Perspective**—The ability to realise that difficult times are mere moments in comparison to your whole lifespan; these moments will pass.
2. **Humility**—The ability to refrain from setting yourself up on a platform you might fall from. To be able to see yourself as one of a billion people all wanting the same thing.
3. **Humour**—Never taking oneself too seriously; to be able to laugh at one's mistakes.
4. **Acceptance**—If you're able to change something, then change it. If not, don't worry about it.
5. **Forgiveness**—There is only pain and suffering for those who can't forgive.
6. **Gratitude**—The ability to be able to see the good in life, because it can always be found.
7. **Compassion**—Your own suffering will fade when you're thinking and caring about someone else.
8. **Generosity**—People are made to be generous and care for others.

As I mentioned, there's extensive overlap between characteristics of a joyful person and that of a self-actualised person. Being self-actualised and being 'the best you can be' sounds hard. Self-actualisation sounds like no small feat, especially when we think of a monk or political figure in history such as Abaraham Lincoln.

We feel that in order to self-actualise, we have to be extraordinary. If we compare the way a self-actualised person approaches life to the way an average person lives life, we find that it is extraordinary. We knew self-actualization would be difficult but most of us probably never thought it would make us happy. Maybe some of us thought that being our best self would make us extraordinary and respected, but not necessarily happy. However, few people realise that being our best self is the pathway to happiness.

Let's look at the overlapping characteristics to see how they are closely linked:

Gratitude / Appreciation

The self-actualised characteristic of **Appreciation** is very similar, if not exactly the same as **Gratitude**, a characteristic of joy. The only difference is that gratitude is more of an emotional response, whereas appreciation is more of an acknowledgement. However, I tend to believe the only difference was the choice of words used.

Humility / Humour / Authenticity

The second similarity is between the self-actualised characteristic of **Authenticity** and the joyful characteristics of **Humility** and **Humour**. Authenticity is the ability to be oneself despite the influence of society and people around you. In Western society, one cannot be humble if they aren't being their authentic self. It goes against the societal message which is to 'flash the cash' and let people know how successful you are. We are being influenced to show off, wear clothes we can't afford, and drive flashy cars that make us look wealthier than we really are. I believe that the only way to be humble is to be your authentic self. Your achievements are not about impressing people or raising your social status. Your skills are simply a means of enhancing your capabilities. By knowing your capabilities, you can be modest because you know what you're good at and you don't need to prove it to anyone. Equally, you know what you're not skilled at and you have the humility to accept that.

The other joyful characteristic is **humour.** The Dalai Lama and Archbishop Tutu said that to really have the characteristic of humour, you have to be at the stage where you can laugh at yourself and your flaws. It takes a lot of self-esteem and self-worth to be able to laugh at yourself. It takes a high level of self-acceptance and self-awareness, which, when fully developed, leads to authenticity. In an indirect way, I would deem humour as a by-product of authenticity. Only when you're truly happy with yourself, can you laugh at yourself without any dent to your self-worth.

Perspective / Equanimity

The self-actualized characteristic of **Equanimity**, the ability to deal with difficulties in a calm manner, is massively related to **perspective,** a characteristic of joy. You can only deal with difficulties in a calm manner once you have perspective. You might have a huge problem at work which is causing you a great deal of stress. However, if you view it with perspective, acknowledging troubles that come along all the time, you'll discover that this is no different to others.

Have you handled difficulties before? Are you just an employee trying your best and using every resource available to try to solve the problem? Will you get another job if you get fired? This situation may be a bit painful, but when you look back at your whole life, will this simply be a side note? These questions will provide perspective and allow you to handle the situation with a sense of equanimity. Put simply, perspective is the skill and equanimity; the outcome.

Compassion / Good moral intuition

The self-actualised characteristic: **good moral intuition** and the characteristic of joy: **compassion** are also closely linked. You can't have one without the other. You can't have good moral intuition without having compassion. If you have compassion, then for the most part, you're probably a moral person. Again, one is the skill and the other (once applied) is the outcome.

This shows that the characteristics of joy and the characteristics of a self-actualised person are really one and the same. The only difference is the choice of words used to convey them. If you want to live a happy and joyful life, you have to strive to be the best person you can be. Choose whichever door (or wording) you want, but they will bring you to the same place.

To develop these characteristics, we need to take ourselves out of our comfort zone. That is what we'll use our bucket list to do.

CHAPTER FIVE

Societal Conditioning and Biology

BEFORE MAKING A BUCKET LIST that will improve your self-development and promote your personal growth, you must know yourself. That is, to **truly** know yourself; your pros, your cons, your hopes and your dreams. You must look at what you're good at and what you're lacking in. You must look at where you are in relation to your life goals and where you want to be. You must ask yourself questions that you've never asked yourself before. Your answers will help you to develop a higher sense of self awareness.

Before we know ourselves, we must find out how we are influenced. Some people believe that we are born with free will and that we choose our fate and destiny. If you believe this then that's great, it's not a bad way to live. At least you believe you have control over your life. Yes, we have free will. We can do things such as fly to Rome in the morning on a whim. However, most of us are not as impulsive even if we want to be. There are many reasons for our lack of impulsivity. We have jobs we can't leave, kids that need to be taken care of and a limited supply of money.

Yes, these are practical reasons but there's even more physiological and sociological reasons for our lack of spontaneity. What else holds back our pursuit of adventure and happiness?

We are significantly affected by what others think and what others do. Self-comparison is one of the biggest predictors of human behaviour. We behave and act the same way as people around us. If the people you associate with take drugs and steal cars, eventually you will do the same. If the people you spend time with buy property and stocks, eventually you will do the same. Jim Rohn famously said: "we are the average of the five people we spend the most time with."

If we have free will, why are we so easily influenced by the people around us? Studies have shown that you are far more likely to engage in criminal activity if the people around you are engaging in this behaviour. This is regardless of race or socioeconomic background. As human beings, we succumb to social influence because we are herd animals. They say being human is being half way between supreme intelligence and an animal. However, as human beings, our narcissism steers us away from our animalistic roots and favours the supreme intelligence perspective. However, humans are herd animals.

During the human evolution process from primate to modern human, we formed tribes, hunting parties and coalitions. The members of these groups worked together to help each other. This occurred because the group enhanced the individual's chances of survival. If the group survived, then the individual survived. The individual benefits by supporting the group, the group reciprocates by supporting the individual. This was formed as a necessity. Human beings don't have the physical attributes to protect themselves efficiently. We have no claws, sharp teeth or thick skin. We needed safety in numbers to survive. Whilst being preyed on by animals with better physical attributes, group cooperation increased the individual's resources. The more people in the group, the more food that could be gathered. The more members involved, the larger the game that could be killed. When someone says: "I don't care what people think," it's most likely a lie.

We have evolved to care about what other people in our group think about us. By caring about what other group members think about you, you're more able to adjust your behaviour to fit into the group. As a result, you'll be liked, your status will be secure and you won't be banished. If other people liked us, then our position in the group would be solidified. That means there's a higher chance of survival. In contrast, if other people in the group didn't like us, we'd be cast into the wilderness and our chances of survival would dramatically decrease.

However, being liked by others is simply not enough for us humans. Humans, like apes, have a need for hierarchy. The higher our social status in the group, the more access to food and resources we would have. The higher our social status, the more desirable we'd be towards the opposite sex. The more resources available, the more likely your offspring would be to survive.

It is in our biology to want to be liked by others and to want to climb the hierarchical ladder. How does this apply to modern times? Even though we are a long way from apes, we are just as likely to conform today as we were in the past.

There was a popular study on conformity called the **Asch conformity paradigm** which was a laboratory experiment to study how and why people conform. It consisted of 50 participants who were assessed doing a 'line judgement task'. They simply looked at lines to see which one was the longest. Asch placed a 'normal' participant in a room with seven confederates. The confederates were planted and agreed in advance what their answers would be when presented with the line task. The real participant (the one being tested) didn't know about the confederates and was led to believe that the other seven confederates were real participants. The answer was always reasonably distinguishable as the longest. The real participant sat at the end of the row and gave their answer last.

There were 18 trials in total, and the confederates gave the wrong answer on 12 trials (called the critical trials). Asch was interested to see if the real participant would conform to the majority view. Asch's experiment also had a control condition where there were no confederates, only a "real participant".

Asch measured the number of times each participant conformed to the majority view. On average, about one third (32%) of the participants who were placed in this situation conformed with the clearly incorrect majority on the critical trials. Over the 12 critical trials, about 75% of participants conformed at least once, and 25% of participants never conformed. In the control group, with no pressure to conform, and only one other person giving the correct answer, less than 1% of participants gave the wrong answer.

Why did the participants conform so readily? When they were interviewed after the experiment, most of them said they didn't really believe their conforming answers, but had gone along with the group for fear of being embarrassed.

They were uncomfortable with disagreeing with the majority. A few of them said that they really did believe the group's answers were correct. Apparently, people conform for two main reasons: because they want to fit in with the group and because they believe the group is smarter than they are.

This human behaviour is best displayed when interacting with children.

"Why did you do that?"

"Everyone else was doing it!"

"Did you think it was a good idea?"

"No, but when the rest of them were doing it, I thought it wasn't so bad".

We even use conformity over our own judgement to prevent us from making positive steps, just because they're not mainstream. For example: "You should really invest in property. On average, property goes up 3% in value every year."

"If it's that great, why isn't everyone doing it?"

We hear this all the time, not just from kids but from ourselves. We must recognise that, in relation to conformity, we haven't changed that much.

We are influenced more than ever now with advertisements plastered over social media, TV and radio. Why are there so many ads? Consumerism is the idea that happiness depends on obtaining goods and material possessions. Marketing targets our animalistic tendencies for societal status. Advertisements convey a fabricated picture that status is obtained by the amount of money you make; that having money and spending it on material possessions will make you happy. This is so far from the truth but it's the societal message being conveyed. Our society is primarily controlled by companies that produce products due to it being a capitalist society. Consumerism uses our animalistic desires (and our need to conform) in order to market their products. This is a very basic description and there's a huge moral debate surrounding this. However, we must acknowledge that society shapes our perspective and values.

In the same way that society shapes us, our nationality shapes our identity and values. As an Irish person travelling abroad, I felt obligated to live up to the stereotype that the Irish are big drinkers and borderline alcoholics! At times I held this flag high and verified the stereotype, but as I grew older and became aware of societal pressure, I didn't feel the need to succumb to it. However, it was only by awareness and conscious action that I was able to achieve this.

To know our true identity and become self-aware, we must acknowledge how we are shaped by our environment. We are shaped by personality, locality, education, our parents, religion and nationality. When making decisions, it's important to at least factor in your biases. It will help you to be more open.

I grew up in rural Ireland countryside where the trend at the time was to build a detached 4-bedroom two story house. I have to factor that bias in when looking at property. Townhouses with close amenities are a better choice, rather than a big house which I don't need nor can afford.

Most importantly, knowing how you are influenced by society is the best way to recognise your own unique identity and become truly self-aware. It will help you to see who you are and what your authentic self looks like. Imagine you grew up in another country with a different religion and your parents were a different socioeconomic class. What attributes do you think would be the same? What values do you think would remain?

As children, we are born as our authentic selves. We don't care what others think about our interests and we don't worry about what is 'cool' or 'uncool'. All we need to know is that our parents care for us and we have food and shelter. That's it. It is through social conditioning (such as schooling and other societal groups) that we're forced to change our behaviour to become part of the group. This is despite the fact that the need of a group for survival is long gone. Imagine your identity is like a mirror: as a child, you were a brand-new mirror and your reflection showed your authentic self. Later, as an adult, after years of neglecting your true self and accumulating influence from society, you become a mirror covered in dust. To find your authentic self again, you must remove the influences of your environment and polish away the dust.

It's important to see how you are personally influenced by your biology, psychology and society as a whole. Be aware of it, notice what goes against your values and try to remove the influence. Do you post pictures just for likes? Did you pick a career for the money and status, rather than for the love of it? Did you choose a boyfriend because your parents would like him, rather than how much you like him?

For those of you who think that we have free will, I disagree. I think that only a few of us have true free will. I believe that the majority of us right now are slaves to our base desires, which are shaped and manipulated by capitalism and consumerism. However, I think that free will can be attained if we recognise how easily we can be conditioned and acknowledge our desire to conform. The old saying: "awareness is half a problem solved" rings true. Once we're aware of how conditioned we are through society, we can learn how to resist and be our true selves.

Resist conformity

The first step to self-awareness is acknowledging that we're not as free minded as we once believed. We must be able to resist the influencers that negatively impact our lives. We must learn not to conform just because *"everyone else is doing it."*

"They must know best."

"I can't be right if I'm going against what the majority is doing."

We must resist conformity so we can be ourselves and be the best we can be. I don't mean that it's necessary to go off the grid and live in a hut in the middle of nowhere, preaching against consumerism and capitalism. That is what Ted Kaczynski, the Unabomber, did.

What I mean is, observe how you are affected by society. Notice the aspects about yourself that you don't like. Actively try to stop doing them. Maybe you're sick of checking your social media fifty times a day and you'd like to reduce your screen time. Maybe you're exhausted from seeking self-worth from strangers online and instead want to seek it from within. Maybe you're tired of the rat race and can't imagine any job you'd want to do for the rest of your life, so you decide to join the F.I.R.E movement (Financially Independent, Retire Early).

There's no-one who sums up non-conformity better than my favourite writer and philosopher Ralph Waldo Emmerson. Emerson wrote his best work in the 1840's. Everything he wrote then is just as applicable today. Emerson said: "Society never advances. It recedes as fast on one side as it gains on the other."

Emerson's view of society is that it may change, but for each positive change there is an equally negative one. The result is always stagnation. Look at society now: we have massive advances in technology. I can use my phone to book a trip around Europe. I can call someone across the world in a matter of seconds. I can look up information almost instantaneously. Despite all these advances, the average person is overweight, impatient, has anxiety issues and is unfulfilled. This is directly related to the advances in society. Young people spend so much time online that they've become anxious about meeting people in person. Fast food is so readily available, that most developed countries have problems with obesity. Finally, because of social media, the standards of self-comparison have gone sky high.

Before, if you were the fastest runner in your parish, you were delighted. Now, you can easily come across someone online (perhaps on the other side of the world), who is faster than you and two years younger. We end up comparing ourselves to people we've never met. The result? A reduced sense of self-worth.

How relative is Emerson's findings 200 years ago, to today?

*The answer is **a lot**.*

It's no measure of health or well-being to adjust to a profoundly unhealthy society. That's not to say that all society is bad. However, taking a promotion, making more money and not seeing your kids much as a result, is probably not that important, according to society's beliefs.

Buying a new car to keep up with the Joneses may only make you compare yourself to every-one else, making you feel less worthy. Begin to have the courage to throw societal norms to the side. Live life according to your own inner morals and motivations. Emerson says: "imitation is suicide" and "Whoso would be a man (or woman), must be a nonconformist". What this means in modern terms is: whoever will be a true authentic person will be a nonconformist. The person who will be the happiest and most personally developed will be someone who can go against the grain, not needing to conform to societal trends. Someone who can entertain the thoughts of the majority without having to accept them as their own truths. When starting to re-evaluate societal norms based on your own values, one must aspire to be a hypocrite. Yes, that's what I said. One must aspire to be a hypocrite, to be a good person and be your best self. You must not be afraid to change your mind.

"Speak what you think today in hard words and tomorrow speak what tomorrow thinks in hard words again, though it contradicts everything you said today."

– Ralph Waldo Emmerson

Don't be afraid to think something that contradicts something you previously believed in the past. Don't be afraid to be a hypocrite as it stops you from progressing, growing and developing. How many hypocrites changed their minds and helped stop apartheid? How many hypocrites changed their minds and helped women seek their right to vote? How many hypocrites changed their minds and abolished slavery?

Don't be afraid to gather new information and change your mind.

Once you remove the fear of hypocrisy, your eyes will be truly opened. Even the fear of hypocrisy is a test of non-conformity. For the most part, we're not afraid to change our mind, but we are afraid of what people will think of us if we change our mind.

Once you have relinquished this fear, you won't be coming into discussions with a strong un-moveable perspective which prevents you from listening to reason. You'll be more open to discussions, listen more and be more objective. You'll be less likely to jump down someone's throat when they say something that you disagree with. Even if they say something that threatens an aspect of your identity such as your favourite sports team or political party. Once you have loosened society's grip on your thoughts and actions, you'll learn to trust your own thoughts. You'll learn how to have a different opinion than the majority and be okay with it. It's okay to be the only vegetarian in the office. It's okay to go on a night out and not drink alcohol. It's okay to be a writer, an artist, a boxer or a Youtuber. Getting to this stage of freedom of thought is one of life's biggest achievements.

"To be yourself in a world that is constantly trying to make you something else is the greatest accomplishment."

– Ralph Waldo Emerson

This is not an easy feat by any means. Often society will whip you with its discontent. For example, I am healthy, train several times a week and watch my weight. However, I don't try to force my beliefs about exercise and healthy diet onto anyone else. I don't know how many times I've brought a healthy packed lunch to work and someone says: "Oh, those grapes are not that healthy you know, they have sugar in them."

First of all, they are very different sugars to those in sweets, but that same person has just told me they had a takeaway pizza the night before! For lunch, they are piling on the carbs with a big bowl of pasta and sinking a red bull even though they've no intention of exercising or burning it off. Yet they comment on my grapes being unhealthy! This happens all the time. By being different, I am making them feel uncomfortable about themselves. As such, they are subconsciously trying to make themselves feel better about it. If you're healthy, you'll often hear people say: "I wish I could eat anything I want just like you". I tell them that if they want to train hard five days a week like me, they can!

This applies to more than health. People who have no clue about stocks or investments will tell you it's very risky to invest in stocks. People will tell you that meditation doesn't work for them, if they find out that you practise it. By being your authentic self, you're more likely different to the average person. The ignorant person may show their displeasure. However, meet their displeasure with a wall of self-belief. Know that:

"To be great is to be misunderstood"

– R.W. Emerson

To be yourself is to be misunderstood by all but those that truly know you.

CHAPTER SIX

Know Thyself

Values, principles, morals

WE HAVE LOOKED AT THE CHARACTERISTICS of self-actualised people and the characteristics of people who want to live a happy and joyful life. We have also looked at how we are built to conform and how we are influenced by society. We know that societal influence may have focused our view externally, rather than on our internal self.

We must look at how societal influence has affected us. By observing self-actualised people, we know where we would like to be. Now we need to look at where we are. We need to truly know ourselves. What are our values, principles and morals? How do my values and morals differ to that of my parents, siblings and partner? What do I value? What is unique to me? Who is in my inner circle? To do this we must examine ourselves.

Why do we need to examine ourselves?

If we want to know how to set bucket list goals that will help us to improve ourselves, we need to gauge where we are currently. For those people who don't know themselves, they not only don't know their present self, but they also don't know who they can become. They do not know their potential self. This applies to most people.

Most people don't know their values or their strongest attributes. Most importantly, they don't even know their weaknesses. These people live an unexamined life and as a result, will have to learn through experience. Unfortunately, they're not confident enough to take risks, fearing they don't have the skills or qualities necessary to succeed. Perhaps they shy away from applying for jobs or taking up certain hobbies. This happened to me.

I thought I wanted to work in HR. After all, given my degree, that was where the money was. It was also one of the few areas a psychology graduate could use their degree in a practical sense, if they didn't want to be a clinical psychologist. I took a job in compliance at a horrible company. I hated it.

I was very anxious and apprehensive working in that company even though I wasn't normally an anxious person. They didn't care about the people they were supposedly trying to help; the company ran on greed. Everyone who worked there was trying to get ahead and make "real money" while being paid a pittance. It was a pit of snakes for someone who didn't value money the same way as the others. It was always going to be a temporary job but it was an experience I could have avoided if I knew myself better.

This mistake occurred due to the fact that I didn't know who I was, nor what I valued. More accurately, I didn't apply my values to my career and as such, I job-hopped when I came out of college. It was six months in one snake-pit before moving on to the next. This mentality can make you feel like a dropout artist. It applies, not just in jobs, but in hobbies and relationships too.

When you become a dropout artist, you lack confidence. You don't know if you can commit to something because you've never been motivated enough to persevere. This can cause its own problems. These are some of the cons of living an unexamined life.

"The unexamined life is not worth living."

– Socrates

These are the words of the famous Greek philosopher from Athens; Socrates (470–399) BC. Socrates is credited as one of the founders of Western philosophy, and the first moral philosopher of the Western ethical tradition of thought.

Socrates stated that if you live by other people's rules and regimes, without examining what you actually want out of your life and relationships, it is detrimental to the self. Socrates wisely stated that most human decisions are motivated by the desire for happiness. Ultimate happiness comes from knowing oneself. The more a person knows themself, the greater his or her ability to make choices that will inevitably bring them true happiness. Socrates claims that there is no greater good than moral self-examination; that a life not morally self-examined is not worth living. The statement that unexamined lives don't have a purpose and shouldn't be lived is harsh and quite frankly, not true. Radical statement aside, there is merit in what he is saying. To make yourself happy you have to truly know yourself.

Socratic Method

To know oneself, one must ask themselves deep questions; about who they are, what they want from themselves and what they want from life. For Socrates, the world was a classroom and he questioned the rich and poor alike. Socrates wanted to discover the ethical truths about people. Socrates asked questions in a method that came to be known as the Socratic Method. The Socratic method is a form of cooperative logical discussion between two or more people. It is based on asking and answering questions to stimulate critical thinking. Its purpose is to draw out ideas as well as conscious and subconscious talks. Sometimes the answers seemed so obvious that it made Socrates' participants look ignorant. This occurs all the time in day-to-day life. How often have you heard someone say: "It's common sense"?

Common sense occurs when the majority of people actually stop and think about a solution to a problem. The consensus of people will come up with a similar answer. The problem is, we often don't take the time to stop and think about the most common things that affect our life. It's common sense to live below our means and not live pay check to pay check. However, some studies have shown that as much as 60% of Americans live pay check to pay check. It's common sense to eat healthy and exercise but western societies are growing obese. It's common sense that considerable amounts of money won't make you happy, especially if you weren't happy before you had the money. Yet we chase money as if it were immortality. Common sense only occurs when you stop and think about that particular question. If not, you'll just follow the societal herd as is in our nature.

Socrates didn't lecture about what he knew, nor did he claim to know more than the common man. In fact, it was quite the opposite. Socrates claimed to be ignorant, yet he was wise because he recognised his own ignorance. I believe Socrates tried to find common sense; to discover how to live the best life and how to translate that into the conscious minds of people. To know ourselves we must have a Socratic meeting of the self and apply common sense to our life. Try to answer these questions below and see what insights they give you into yourself and life in general.

Sample questions for self-examination:

What are my top 5 values?

_____

_____

_____

What are my top 5 attributes?

_____

_____

_____

What are my top 5 flaws?

_____

_____

_____

What harsh truths do I prefer to ignore about myself?

_____

_____

_____

What do I want out of life?

_____

_____

_____

Where does my self-worth come from?

_____

_____

_____

How often do I lie to myself and others?

_____

_____

_____

How much does fear and anxiety affect my decision making?

_____

_____

_____

What is my greatest fear?

_____

_____

_____

What are the most important decisions I will make in my life?

_____

_____

_____

How do I want to be remembered after I die?

_____

_____

_____

What is my biggest success in life so far? What is my biggest failure in life so far? What have I learned from both?

_____

_____

_____

What is the best way for me to attain happiness?

_____

_____

_____

If I had to guess, what would be the most likely way I will die?

_____

_____

_____

Do I want to be intelligent or would I rather be wise?

_____

_____

_____

By what standards do I judge myself?

_____

_____

_____

What am I capable of achieving?

_____

_____

_____

What activities cause me to feel like I'm living life to the fullest?

_____

_____

_____

What percentage of my life do I truly feel alive? When do I feel that way? How can I feel that way more often?

_____

_____

_____

Philosophical questions

What should be the goal of humanity?

_____

_____

_____

Is 'free will' real or not?

_____

_____

_____

Is there a meaning to life? If so, what is my purpose in life?

_____

_____

_____

What does it mean to live a good life?

_____

_____

_____

How will humans as a species go extinct?

_____

_____

_____

What makes a person human?

_____

_____

_____

Do we need religion to live a moral life?

_____

_____

_____

Is suffering a necessary part of the human condition? What would someone who has never suffered be like?

_____

_____

_____

Does hardship make a person stronger? If so, under what conditions, and at what point, is too much hardship? If not, what makes a person stronger?

If freedom is simply being able to do what you want, are animals freer than humans?

Would you want to know you are going to die beforehand or would you rather die suddenly without warning?

Is it more important to help yourself or others?

What life-altering events should every human ideally get to experience at least once in their lives?

Can human nature be changed? Should it be changed?

_____

_____

_____

Why do we judge ourselves by our intentions but judge others by their actions?

_____

_____

_____

What would I change genetically about humans to make them a better species?

_____

_____

_____

What is the biggest waste of human potential?

_____

_____

_____

Is a life that focuses on avoiding pain and seeking out pleasure a good and worthwhile life? Why or why not?

_____

_____

_____

Does jealousy have value in driving humans to improve themselves or is it a purely negative emotion?

_____

_____

_____

Is happiness just chemicals flowing through your brain or something more?

_____

_____

_____

Why do humans have such a strong urge to distract themselves from the real world?

_____

_____

_____

If you can save another's life, but don't because doing so would break the law, are you ethically justified in your decision?

_____

_____

_____

What is the most fertile soil for hatred? Fear, ignorance, jealousy, or something else entirely?

_____

_____

_____

What would utopia be like? How would it function and continue to exist?

_____

_____

_____

Is hierarchy necessary for all successful human communities?

_____

_____

_____

By completing these questions, you have had a Socratic meeting of the self. Congratulations, you have asked yourself some hard questions. Hopefully you will have a better understanding of yourself; what you think and believe about your capabilities, and how you view life. Now, let's see what standards you live your life by and what you, as an individual, value in life. You may ask what are values?

Values

Values are attributes or characteristics that we hold in high regard. Values are specific to the individual. Most people have similar morals and principles. For example: it's wrong to kill, steal or con someone. These tend to be universal across cultures and demographics, however values are attributes that we have individually. For example, if a person is an artist, they may value creativity, whereas I personally don't value this. I value practicality as I am a practical person. There is no right or wrong value, just different values.

We are all made up of numerous values, but you can tell a lot about yourself if you can identify your top five values. Values affect all aspects of one's life. For example, I value loyalty very highly. Unconsciously, I sought friendships and relationships with people who also value loyalty. I wasn't aware of this until I recognised my values. Values not only affect our friendships, but they also affect our decision making.

We're more likely to make choices that support our value systems rather than not. For example, security could be a strong value for an individual, which many people would have. Say an individual is looking for a job and considering two very similar organisations. Given the choice, the person will most likely go for the one with higher job security over the one that promotes professional development or opportunity for career growth. Another candidate who values achievement may go for the organisation with better career development opportunities. As conveyed in this example, values are not just attributes we like in other people. Values are our own guide post and reward systems for making our decisions. We often value different things than others.

My father grew up on a farm. Few people at that time could afford education, so he values security, especially financial security. He also values education because he didn't have the opportunity to progress past second level education. This is often the case. We tend to value attributes that we lacked in earlier relationships or circumstances.

I have worked in the youth sector for several years, in both a formal and a voluntary capacity. I often meet young people who have been put into foster care. Due to their upbringing, they tend to strongly value attributes such as honesty, loyalty, fairness and accomplishment. Their biological parents were often addicts or suffered from mental health problems. Unfortunately, they were more loyal to substances they were addicted to. Never honest, they were always trying to hide their addiction. Due to this unstable environment, these young people had very different lives to that of a normal person their age. As a result, they felt that life was unfair.

However, you don't need to have a traumatic past in order to value aspects of your life. It could be something smaller that motivates you. Perhaps your parents didn't communicate clearly with you and as a result, you value communication, especially with your partner.

Our chosen values don't have to be due to aspects we lacked in earlier life. However, in the main, these do tend to be higher prioritised values.

Some chosen values are relative to **personality characteristics**. For example, if you're an extrovert, you may value freedom of speech or companionship, whereas an introvert may value personal space and seclusion. Your personality will greatly affect your values.

Finally, your values will be affected by your **upbringing and personal experience**. For example, if you come from a family of doctors and high achievers, you will most likely value achievement. If you come from a family of charity workers and volunteers, you will more than likely value humanitarianism.

Values are attributes we hold in high regard. They help us choose our friends and the people we love. They help us choose life decisions that will make us happier. They affect our attitudes and behaviour. Values are passed on from our parents. Values are influenced by present society. They are also formed through our personality and attributes we felt were missing in life, with most being formulated in childhood. We cannot be our best self without knowing our values. We cannot have a fulfilled and happy existence without living a life that is congruent with our values.

Please see the shortlist of values below and consider which appeals to you:

Acceptance	Clever	Dependability
Accomplishment	Comfort	Determination
Accountability	Commitment	Development
Accuracy	Common sense	Devotion
Achievement	Communication	Dignity
Adaptability	Community	Discipline
Alertness	Compassion	Discovery
Altruism	Competence	Drive
Ambition	Concentration	Effectiveness
Amusement	Confidence	Efficiency
Assertiveness	Connection	Empathy
Attentive	Consciousness	Empower
Awareness	Consistency	Endurance
Balance	Contentment	Energy
Beauty	Contribution	Enjoyment
Boldness	Control	Enthusiasm
Bravery	Conviction	Equality
Brilliance	Cooperation	Ethical
Calm	Courage	Excellence
Candour	Courtesy	Experience
Capable	Creation	Exploration
Careful	Creativity	Expressive
Certainty	Credibility	Fairness
Challenge	Curiosity	Family
Charity	Decisive	Famous
Cleanliness	Decisiveness	Fearless
Clear	Dedication	Feelings

Ferocious	Innovation	Passion
Fidelity	Inquisitive	Patience
Focus	Insightful	Peace
Foresight	Inspiring	Performance
Fortitude	Integrity	Persistence
Freedom	Intelligence	Playfulness
Friendship	Intensity	Poise
Fun	Intuitive	Potential
Generosity	Joy	Power
Genius	Justice	Present
Giving	Kindness	Productivity
Goodness	Knowledge	Professionalism
Grace	Lawful	Prosperity
Gratitude	Leadership	Purpose
Greatness	Learning	Quality
Growth	Liberty	Realistic
Happiness	Logic	Reason
Hard work	Love	Recognition
Harmony	Loyalty	Recreation
Health	Mastery	Reflective
Honesty	Maturity	Respect
Honour	Meaning	Responsibility
Hope	Moderation	Restraint
Humility	Motivation	Results-oriented
Humour	Openness	Reverence
Imagination	Optimism	Rigour
Improvement	Order	Risk
Independence	Organisation	Satisfaction
Individuality	Originality	Security

Self-reliance	Status	Tranquillity
Selfless	Stewardship	Transparency
Sensitivity	Strength	Trust
Serenity	Structure	Trustworthy
Service	Success	Truth
Sharing	Support	Understanding
Significance	Surprise	Uniqueness
Silence	Sustainability	Unity
Simplicity	Talent	Valour
Sincerity	Teamwork	Victory
Skill	Temperance	Vigour
Skillfulness	Thankful	Vision
Smart	Thorough	Vitality
Solitude	Thoughtful	Virtue
Spirit	Timeliness	Wealth
Spirituality	Tolerance	Welcoming
Spontaneous	Toughness	Winning
Stability	Traditional	Wisdom

Now that you've had a look at the list of values, take a moment to consider which appeals to you. Start by **selecting 10 values** that resonate with you. Picking ten values will make it a lot easier before narrowing down again.

_____

_____

_____

When you have your **top 10**, then decide on your **top 5**.

_____

_____

_____

Once you have your **top 5**, rank them in order, with your top value being **number 1**.

_____

_____

_____

Ask yourself: why is this my top value?

_____

_____

_____

Why is this my second top value?

_____

_____

_____

Why is this my third top value?

_____

_____

_____

Why is this my fourth top value?

_____

_____

_____

Why is this my fifth top value?

_____

_____

_____

Then, for each value, ask yourself: **Where did this value come from?**

Did my parents pass this value on to me? Have I chosen this because it relates to my personality type? Is this value due to something that was lacking in my life?

_____

_____

_____

Then ask yourself: How does this value affect my attitude and behaviour in day-to-day life? How does this value affect my decision making?

_____

_____

_____

Once you have answered these questions for all your top 5 values, you will know yourself better than you've ever done.

Now that you know your top values, you can think about your life and contemplate if there's anything you're currently doing that goes against your values?

For example, perhaps your job as a corporate lawyer goes against your top value of fairness. With that in mind, perhaps it would be wise to consider going into a different area of law.

Perhaps your weekend shifts at work clash with the family values you hold dear. You don't have to make changes straight away to accommodate your values, however, awareness of a problem is half a problem solved.

If, however, you're aware of how your lifestyle clashes with your values, yet no changes are made, it will eventually cause great unhappiness. Unhappiness is a result of someone living a life not congruent with their values.

If you notice any big conflicts between your lifestyle and your values, it's a good idea to put an item on your bucket list that will challenge that area of your life, aligning it with your values.

Perhaps you need to change your career to coincide with your values. Perhaps you need to remove people from your inner circle who don't share your values or who have a negative effect on you. Perhaps you need to take up a hobby that allows you to express a certain value.

Include your values when making decisions. For example, does this company share my values or should I do business elsewhere? Does this college course allow me to channel my values or is the end goal simply about financial benefit? Any items that exhibit your values are well deserving of your bucket list.

CHAPTER SEVEN

Values and psychological needs

ONCE I DISCOVERED MY VALUES, I felt like I gained a lot of clarity in my life. I knew what I liked and didn't like. I knew that living a life which coincided with my values was the path to happiness. I changed my job from compliance and human resources to working with young people and youth work. I stopped playing hurling and took up boxing, which was a sport I always wanted to do. I started pursuing women who shared my values.

All these decisions changed my life for the better but they were slow and I didn't make them all at once. These decisions occurred over the course of three years. Each decision was the catalyst for the next.

However, there were some things I didn't understand about values and for the life of me, I didn't know why. I didn't understand the variance in people's values throughout their lifetime. It wasn't until I listened to Tony Robbins that I could understand. Tony talked about the six psychological needs of people. My values are

From Bucket List To Best Self

similar to people my own age and differ to those who are older than me. I started to appreciate what my dad meant when he said: "You'll understand when you are older."

The six psychological needs of people are:

- Certainty
- Variety
- Significance
- Love/ connection
- Personal growth
- Contribution to something more

Certainty relates to the level of security and routine someone needs in their life in order to feel safe. For example, how much do you need in your bank account to feel safe? How willing are you to find a part-time job alongside college in order to give you a sense of security? If raised by unreliable parents, do you like to surround yourself with extremely reliable people? Everyone has their own level of certainty. This is the level of conscious action that a person needs to take as preventative action against their fears. For example, if a person is afraid of losing their job and not being able to pay their mortgage, they should take out mortgage payment protection insurance. Certainty defines the level of control you need in your life.

The second need is that of **Variety** (or uncertainty). How much change do you need in your life? Do you need to have trips planned or are you a spontaneous traveller? Do you have that one friend who is unpredictable? How much variance or uncertainty do you need in your life? How much adventure do you need in your life?

The third psychological need is **significance**: To what extent (and in what area of your life) do you want to feel important? Is it in your job? In your volunteering? In your family? In your sport? Everybody wants to feel significant to a certain degree. Some need to have important jobs and titles, others need personal achievements and recognition. Some just need to be important to a small circle of people in their life.

Tony Robbins advised that these three psychological needs were in the first tier. They were more prominent (and first addressed) during a younger person's development. The second tier, consisting of the following three psychological needs, often become addressed as we get older, past the youthful stage of mid-to-late twenties.

However, in this changing of the guard from the first tier to the second tier, the levels of need in the first stage often change. For example, older people often need less variance and more certainty than that of young people. Older people may have a higher need for significance than younger people.

Love and connection are within the second tier. We all need to feel love or connected to people, whether this is a friendship or a romantic partner. Even priests and monks who have forsaken romantic love and procreation need to feel connected to their congregation or community.

Then, there is the need for **personal growth.** Sometimes people mask their need for significance, status or ego by claiming they're working on personal growth. For example, a wealthy surgeon could be informed that his bedside manner is very cold. He thinks "What do they know? I make £300k per year saving people's lives. What does it matter about bedside manner?" This shows huge significance and ego, yet an absolute avoidance of personal growth. Most people have an inbuilt need for personal growth; to become happier and not repeat past mistakes.

Finally, the need to **contribute to something more.** We all have an inner need to contribute to something outside ourselves. Some of us fill this void by having kids. Others by volunteering, such as training local sports clubs. We have a need (subconscious or conscious) to contribute to something in the world, that is more than our own needs. We want to contribute to a cause that will outlive us, a legacy we can leave behind, something that will ultimately still be there when we are gone.

To recap, by now you have looked at how society has influenced you and the aspects of your life you would like to change. You have looked at your values and how they affect your attitude, behaviour, friends and decisions.

Now, take a look at your psychological needs. Observe what you need from your life right now. Notice how that might change in the future.

Personally, I have certainty in my life, such as having absolute trust in my partner and obtaining a degree. I've worked my way up to a middle management position, acquiring a certain level of experience that provides me with a job of suitable pay.

I also need a lot of variety, preferably an annual holiday to a destination with a different culture, new sights and fresh experiences. I need to be constantly trying to improve myself and push myself out of comfort zones. I need to challenge myself and try to conquer my fears.

I have a medium-to-low level of significance. I need to be able to tell people what I do and not be embarrassed about it. I need to have achieve-ments in my life; professional, personal and sporting. I have a high need for love and connect-edness. I need to feel connected to a small group of friends and feel loved by them. I need to feel loved by my partner.

I have a high level for personal growth. I need to feel like I am growing as a person and not making the same mistakes I did in the past.

Finally, I have a medium level for contributing to something more. I need to feel like I'm helping people around me. My job lets me help young people and contribute to their lives. I help my friends personally and emotionally as much as I can. I try to help people where possible. I try to inject a bit more goodness in the world. These are my needs at present but I imagine they will change.

My need for variety will probably reduce as I get older but it'll probably always be a bit higher than normal. As we grow older, there's more emphasis on the second tier than the first, which is natural.

Find out what your level of need is now. Then, try to live life based on your needs and values. Observe what your needs are and to what degree they are. Are your needs high, medium or low? Do you want to increase or decrease them?

Then link your level of psychological need with your top five values. Ask yourself:

Does your life express your values and the degree of psychological needs you have in each area?

This will give you more insight into your self-awareness which will ultimately enhance your life.

Are there any aspects of your life that need to be changed in order for you to live a life that is congruent with your values and psychological needs?

Then those aspects must be put on your bucket list.

CHAPTER EIGHT

Your Life's Purpose

YOU MIGHT WONDER ABOUT the relevance of 'your life's purpose' in relation to a bucket list. Actually, this is one of the most important chapters in the whole book. Most human beings that have accomplished amazing feats (via sport, philanthropy, political or self-actualization) said they felt it was their life's purpose. Most amazing feats were accomplished by someone who had an unwavering purpose and shared it with others. Their purpose, combined with talent, consistency and resilience, is a force of nature.

For example, most people know that Thomas Edison invented the light bulb. However, most people don't know that he had one hundred failed attempts beforehand. However, Edison had a purpose: to better the whole world with his inventions. This purpose allowed him to persist when many others would quit. With his talent and perseverance, he succeeded. His success changed the lives of people from then on.

I had never thought about my life's purpose and I'm sure most people haven't. It was my belief that gifted people would get a calling; that their purpose would be thrust upon them. For example, Nelson Mandela or Muhammad Gandhi. To me, it seemed as though these two men were so consistent and unwavering, the choice to quit must have been non-existent. This, combined with their potential and ability not to conform to society, allowed them to pursue their calling with a vigour most others couldn't.

In my early twenties, it was my belief that only prodigies have callings. Even though I was becoming a more well-rounded person, I was by no means a prodigy. I'm still not. Like most young people, I dismissed the notion of having a life's purpose. I thought no further than having a realistic career with a decent income; a job that would hopefully have some intrinsic value. I hoped that if I helped others in some capacity, that would bring some level of intrinsic value. Even by this limited emotional thinking, I felt I was ahead of the game. Most people my age just wanted money and status. I wanted money too, but the thought of doing a job I hated for the rest of my life saddened me. So, I decided to sacrifice the extent of financial reward in return for something I enjoyed.

By this time, I was finishing my Masters in the University College of Cork where I was studying Positive Psychology and Executive Coaching. I told my parents that as soon as I had finished, I was going to travel around Europe. I spouted off a list of countries I would visit. I told them all about my bucket list and each place I planned to see. I mentioned that I was going to visit Krakow in Poland and I was going to do a day trip to Auschwitz, the concentration camp.

As a result of this conversation, my mother gave me a short 100-page book about an Auschwitz survivor. The book was called: "Man's Search for Meaning" written by Viktor E. Frankl. Little did my mother know, she had given me a book that would change my view on the world and my place in it forever.

The book detailed how Viktor Frankl endured the concentration camp. He described the elements he needed to endure it. He also portrayed what was left in a human being after they've been stripped of everything else. While in the concentration camp, Frankl was subjected to many forms of torture, both physical and mental. In spite of the enforced physical and mental primitiveness of life in a concentration camp, Frankl believed it was possible for a spiritual person to deepen and expand. He said this was evident when people from higher economic backgrounds were able to acclimatise to camp life better than those who were used to working in more labour-intensive jobs. This, he believed, was due to some people's ability to retreat from their terrible surroundings to a life of inner riches and spiritual freedom. Frankl believed this was the only way one could explain the apparent paradox that some prisoners of affluent backgrounds often seemed to survive camp life better than those of labour-intensive backgrounds despite the work relating more to their experience.

Frankl describes such days when the camp workers were woken before sunrise, stumbling through darkness, over mountains and through streams in freezing conditions. The accompanying guards would be shouting at them and driving the butts of their rifles into any men who fell behind. Anyone who had very sore feet supported themself on his neighbour's arm. Hardly a word was spoken while working. The icy wind did not encourage talk. Once they returned to camp, they were given rations that wouldn't nourish a child, never mind a grown man who's just done a day's labour. Slowly, they drained away, with many succumbing to disease or starvation.

Frankl stated that while he was forced to work, he would spend the day talking to his wife. It was his way of coping with the suffering he was being subjected to. He would spend hours talking to her as though she was there beside him, replying back to him. He often discussed with her about the meaning of why he was subjected to such suffering. His revelation was best described by him in the following extract from his book:

"Death came swiftly to him who saw no more sense in his life, no aim, no purpose, and therefore no point in carrying on. He was soon lost. The typical reply with which such a man rejected all encouraging arguments was, "I have nothing to expect from life anymore." What sort of answer can one give to that? What was really needed was a fundamental change in their attitude toward life. They had to learn by themselves and, furthermore, they had to teach the despairing men that it didn't really matter what they expected from life, but rather what life expected from them. To survive they needed to stop asking about the meaning of life, and instead to think of themselves as those who were being questioned by life daily and hourly. Life ultimately means taking the responsibility to find the right answer to its problems and to fulfil the tasks which it constantly sets for each individual. These tasks, and therefore the meaning of life, differ from man to man, and from moment to moment. Thus it is impossible to define the meaning of life in a general way. Questions about the meaning of life can never be answered by sweeping statements. "Life" does not mean something vague, but something very real and concrete, just as life's tasks are also very real and concrete. They form man's

destiny, which is different and unique for each individual. No man and no destiny can be compared with any other man or any other destiny. No situation repeats itself, and each situation calls for a different response. Sometimes the situation in which a man finds himself may require him to shape his own fate by action. At other times it is more advantageous for him to make use of an opportunity for contemplation and reflection. Sometimes man may be required simply to accept fate, to bear his cross. Every situation is distinguished by its uniqueness."

What Frankl is saying is that we expect a lot from life. We expect to be happy, we expect to have secure jobs and become wealthy. We expect a nice car and a nice house, to be well dressed and have polite, capable kids. This is what we expect from life. Frankl believes that people who think like this are more prone to despair as once these goals are accomplished then these people have nothing to live for. This can be replicated in people who only want to be happy. They just want to feel good about themselves every day. How realistic is this? Happiness is not always in our control. We cannot feel good about ourselves or about what we do at all times because external forces can make us feel bad about them. In other words, life makes us feel bad about them. We do something wrong at work; we feel bad, we give our children inadequate advice; we feel bad, our neighbour gets a nicer car than us; we feel bad. Happiness is an emotion and our emotions are affected by our interactions.

In addition to life hampering our happiness, we are subject to the "Law of Familiarity". The Law of Familiarity is based on the concept that when you experience something enough times, it becomes familiar to you. You become desensitised to its positive effects and experience less gratitude for it. This could relate to a person, a place or an experience.

This concept can be depicted by a romantic relationship. At the start of the relationship, couples are loving and appreciative of each other. How they may relate to each other five years later, could be a different story. The same goes with a new car. When you first purchase it, you might ensure it is valeted regularly and you take it to the car wash weekly. If anything's wrong with it, you take it to the mechanic straight away. Two years later, you might forget to get it serviced on time. My point is, that no matter what we get, we will want more. After a certain period of time, it will no longer satisfy us. It's in our nature. That's why Olympians strive for several gold medals rather than settling for just one. It's the reason why some millionaires own several companies. It's not because they needed them, it's because they're no longer satisfied with running one company or winning one gold medal.

In the early ages, that was very useful for us. It meant that we explored the world and strived for a better quality of life. However, it also makes contentment very difficult. This lack of contentment can be counteracted however by doing some gratitude work, which will be discussed later in this book.

With this in mind, we can only conclude that "striving for happiness" doesn't make sense. Happiness is an emotion. Emotions are not stable; they change depending on one's interaction with life and with their current thoughts. Emotions are forever changing because life is forever changing.

You can't be happy forever, no more than you can be angry forever. Happiness is the most desired emotion, however, contrary to popular opinion, it is not a destination. "One day, I'll be happy and then I'll be happy from then on." No, one day you'll be happy and the next you won't. The next day you might be happy in the morning, then sad in the evening. Don't strive for something that is unobtainable. Consistent happiness is impossible. Just as we can't stop the world from spinning on its axis, we can't stop our emotions from changing. Happiness shouldn't be seen as a destination. Rather, it is an outcome of living life in a manner that is congruent with our morals and values. Happiness comes with a sense of achievement when we triumph over life's tasks and milestones. Happiness is a moving goal post which most people aim for.

What should I aim for with my life, if not happiness? You should strive for a life's purpose. You should strive for your purpose in life that is specific to you alone.

What is a life's purpose?

The Oxford dictionary describes purpose as: "the reason something is done or created or for which something exists."

Some people say it's the reason you were put on this planet or the reason you were born. If you have a life purpose, your task will be to direct the intentionality of your life towards it. It will be the force behind your resolve and determination. In essence, a life purpose is a never-ending goal you want to achieve within your lifetime.

A life's purpose could be wanting to help as many victims as possible through domestic abuse. It could be trying to counteract climate change, like Greta Thunberg. It could be as simple as being known as a respectable and honourable man in the community.

We need a purpose to give us direction and perspective in life. Otherwise, it's very easy to get sucked into a life's purpose dictated by social norms or societal trends. For example: *"Become rich and famous, buy as many material positions as you can; that will make you happy."*

Discovering your life's purpose makes you see what you **really** want from life. It stops you from getting caught up in outside pressures. It prevents you from having to learn from experience about what is important and what isn't.

A life's purpose works best when it involves helping people in some shape or form. This is because we are herd animals and helping others makes us intrinsically happy.

Secondly, it works best when it is lifelong. Sometimes people have a very noble life's purpose, such as being the best mother to their children. That is admirable, but what happens when your children grow up, become independent and fly the nest? Then what do you do? You're left meandering, lacking purpose and fulfilment. I understand that a mother will always be a mother, but not to the same extent as being a protective, providing figure to young children.

Try, if possible, to find a purpose (or goal) that will help others and is lifelong. It's no easy feat!

To formulate your life's purpose can take years. No one else can help you with it.

> *"Each man (or woman) is questioned by life; and he/she can only answer to life by answering for their own life."*
>
> *– Viktor Frankl*

We can only live our best life once we have something to strive for; something that is not shaken by our meagre wants and trivialities, something that is specific to us as an individual. A purpose can anchor your personal ascension to the sky and give you somewhere to aim. No one can tell you what your purpose is, and even when you decide on your purpose, it might change as time goes on.

For example, Bill Gates' purpose was to have the internet accessible to everyone. He wanted everyone to have a computer on their desk. He believed that it would improve mankind if they had access to knowledge at their fingertips. Years later and mission accomplished, his purpose has evolved. Now he wants to help prevent unnecessary deaths in third world countries due to people drinking dirty water. Bill Gates may not have expected to complete his life's purpose to the extent that he did, however once he did, his purpose changed. It changed but it is still the same, to improve mankind.

Even though I mentioned that a purpose should be lifelong, we should be open to change. You might discover that your original purpose is not for you. Or you might change your opinion on what your purpose is. Bill Gates' purpose changed but he continued to apply himself, working towards the best that he could be.

No one can tell you what your purpose should be. However, some people believe that a purpose can only be effective if it involves some capacity to help your fellow man. Only then, can your purpose provide worth, direction and inner resolve. I believe this to be true. If your purpose is based on extrinsic values, you'll never be motivated enough to follow through. You need to be driven by a purpose that will motivate you to persevere in the face of adversity.

When I first heard about the idea of a life's purpose, I found the concept very difficult to grasp. I assumed that the greatest thing we could strive for was happiness. I never considered that there could be more to it than that. Nor did I take into account that happiness is changeable and therefore can't be a destination. I thought about it for days.

At the age of twenty-two, I conceded that everything in my life had been selfishly driven in one way or another. Like many others my age, I was self-absorbed. I did everything for myself and no one else. My sports goals were to feel good. My college goals were to get an education. My education goals were to get a good job. My plan to go travelling to San Francisco and work on building sites was my opportunity to have one last 'piss-up' before growing up.

Even my choice of degree was selfish. Studying Psychology, which most people would assume is about helping others, wasn't chosen for that purpose. Instead, I chose psychology because I wanted answers to all my "Why" questions.

- Why are some people erratic and lack the capacity for emotional depth?
- Why is my friend depressed when he is smart, good looking, athletic and always has a girlfriend?
- Why am I so different from my siblings?
- How does my father keep it all together?

Yes, even my degree choice was selfish.

I thought back to the times I had helped others. I have fond memories of training the under 18's and under 21's at hurling. Even though I was only a year older than the under 21's, I really enjoyed training the young men and watching them develop under my instruction. I thought back to when I volunteered at a youth club and how rewarding it was to help young people stay on the right path. So, I decided I was going to do youth work.

Unfortunately, there were no opportunities for youth work in the area at the time. Instead, I worked with autistic adults who had challenging behaviour. I worked in that job for nearly two years. My heart wasn't in it but I learned a lot and it prepared me for a future job managing a youth charity in the Midwest of Ireland. In that role, it confirmed how much I love working with young people.

However, as I develop, I'm learning that I want to do more than helping young people out of crisis. Rather than just help people survive, I want to help people thrive. To be the best that they can be. I have always wanted to live my best life; not to waste a single day. I always wanted to excel at sport, get a degree and see as much of the world as I could. However, despite my burning desire to help others, it became apparent that I can't help others without helping myself first. To show someone how to be the best they can be, I need to try to do the same thing myself.

It was at this moment that my bucket list changed from being a list of places to visit, to a strategic plan to develop as a person. It became a way of forcing me out of my comfort zone. The first, and most important thing you should have on your bucket list is to find your purpose in life. It doesn't have to be the first task you complete. The more you experience, the more knowledgeable you'll be towards recognising your purpose. Your bucket list will lead you to your purpose. Once you find your purpose, pursue it with as much passion and consistency as you can. Your life will change for the better.

Note: I'm definitely not suggesting that in order to find your purpose, you need to quit your job and work in a caring profession. Depending on your personality, that mightn't make financial (or even emotional) sense.

Take my boxing coach, for example. He works in a biomedical company as a line manager. However, his purpose in life is to promote the name of the boxing club that has been in his family for three generations. It doesn't pay the bills. In fact, it actually takes money out of his own pocket. However, he wants to produce the best amateur boxing champions and he wants his club to be recognised as one of the best in his country. In doing this, he helps to keep young people off the streets and on the right path. He offers guidance and advice for troubled youths. He brings them on trips abroad and tries to give them good memories. This is a shining example of someone's purpose; to enhance their club, maintain the family name and enhance the lives of people around him.

Note, he didn't quit his job. Nor does he force his purpose onto anyone else.

Your purpose doesn't have to be all-consuming, but it does have to exist.

If you don't have a place to be, any road will bring you there but most roads lead nowhere. You need a purpose so that you don't wander aimlessly in the sea of wants, desires and human nature.

As I explore my purpose, it continues to evolve, however by having a purpose, it gives me immeasurable direction and resilience.

You may ask: how does a purpose in life give you a higher sense of resilience?

- It does this by giving your life meaning.

Once your life has meaning, your existence itself has some intrinsic value and seems a lot brighter. Your life has direction and goals. Once your life has meaning, you're able to deal with suffering that little bit easier.

Frankl stated: "suffering ceases to be suffering at the moment it finds meaning."

That can be a hard concept to comprehend, so let's look at an everyday example.

Let's say there's a young girl in secondary school. She has wandered aimlessly through life, doesn't care about school and isn't interested in any sports. School finishes and she finds a job. It's the first job she can find, one that she isn't interested in, but it pays the bills. She moves out of her parents' house even though it doesn't make financial sense. She spends the next few years drinking and partying. She takes drugs occasionally and has several sexual partners. This young woman doesn't feel like she has a purpose in life. She has no goal to strive for to give her life direction. She doesn't feel that her life can bring much good to others so she doesn't really try. In addition to this, she feels she's not capable of fulfilling society's goals such as becoming wealthy, getting a good degree, or finding a stable job.

She falls pregnant and falls in love with her baby. For the first time in her life, she has a purpose. She has something that she cherishes above her own needs and desires. From then on, her purpose is to be the best mother she can be for her baby. She removes friends who have a negative influence on her life. She returns to education when the child is old enough to go to school. She changes her life around.

That same young woman who never turned up for a class on time, is able to get up at 4am for morning feeds. She works extra shifts in order to be able to buy nice clothes for her child. She handles the burden of being a single parent. She is able to bear the stress and strain of everyday life because she has a purpose. She has meaning. Stress that may have previously set her off on a two-day drinking session, is now bearable as she doesn't have a choice. You might say: "Well, of course she would change. It's different when it's your own child."

Indeed, there is a biological desire to love your child. However, we've all heard of parents who haven't matured, no matter how many children they have. People with a purpose can withstand significant adversity. Not only can they withstand adversity, but they can achieve amazing feats.

"A man or woman with a 'WHY' can accomplish almost any 'HOW'."

The example above shows that someone's purpose can (and often does) change. Being a mother brings great meaning and purpose, however once the children are raised, there could be a feeling of worthlessness. That is, of course, unless one doesn't find a new purpose. It's important to find a new purpose, especially if you want happy, emotionally stable adult children.

This can be a common problem for devoted mothers, especially stay-at-home mothers. When their children no longer need them, they feel lost and worthless. Their purpose has gone. It's useful to recognise, not only what your purpose is, but when you need to change it. It's great that we get to choose our purpose. Also, at any instant, we can change it. There's a sense of freedom and liberation that comes from knowing you can, not only choose your own purpose, but can also change it.

Although a purpose can change, it shouldn't be something that changes every few weeks, months or even years. Your purpose should be something you want to achieve with your life. During the course of your life, you might want to achieve a slightly different purpose. It's perfectly acceptable to adjust one's purpose based on personal experience, but it shouldn't be changed just because of boredom or feeling like the progress is too slow. A purpose is a process, not a destination.

Take, for example, my coach. His purpose was to build the legacy of his boxing club. If one of his fighters becomes a top professional and leaves the club (which has happened in the past), that doesn't mean his purpose has ended.

One of his boxers moved to America and became a world middleweight champion. However, the coach didn't stop working on his gym. He kept training more young people. His purpose was bigger than just one success. A purpose works outside the realm of success and happiness. The more you aim for success and happiness, the more you miss it. Success, like happiness, cannot be pursued, it must ensue. Success and happiness are a process, not a destination. They are a by-product (or side effect) of personal dedication to a purpose greater than oneself.

Success and happiness are subjective to every individual. What you define as success may not be the same for someone else.

Have you ever been in the same room as someone who is very successful? Did you feel worthless in comparison? You were content with your own level of success until you met someone who was even more successful than you. The comparison made your own feelings of success plummet. The same occurs with happiness. You are happy until the sun goes away, the rain falls or you get a flat tyre. Why strive for something so unstable?

Even if we acquire success and happiness, the law of familiarity will make them fade into existence.

To quote Jim Carrey:

"I think everybody should get rich and famous, and do everything they ever dreamed of, so they can see that it's not the answer."

If he's not happy with success and money, then that shows that happiness and success is not something to strive for. Strive for a purpose.

Most people go through life, get an education, and get a job. They might hate the job or they might be indifferent to it. They chase a promotion in search of success, happiness and self-worth. Perhaps they get to their forties or fifties and realise that the money isn't as important. Perhaps the house is nearly paid off and their kids have gone to college. When people get to this stage, they often change professions. They might choose a helping profession or they might follow a passion.

It's at this point that they say they're much happier. They have more time on their hands and they don't even miss the money. This is not true for everyone of course. There are some people who work in careers that they love for their whole life. I am delighted for them. In my experience this is not the norm.

However, if you identify more with the first version, then listen to Frankl's words of wisdom once more:

"Live as if you were living already for the second time and as if you had acted the first time as wrongly as you are about to act now."

In other words, live as though you have wasted the last 50 years chasing success and happiness and now you want to change. It doesn't have to be an extreme change. However, by making small changes as thin as the width of a page every day, that will build up to the width of a book in a year. After several years, you will have something that could stop a bullet. In summary, before completing your bucket list, it's important to find your purpose.

CHAPTER NINE

Fear

"Man's immortality is not to live forever; for that wish is born of fear. Each moment we are free from fear we are immortal."

– Mary Renault

A BUCKET LIST HELPS YOU to become the best person you can be and as close to self-actualisation as possible. The process forces you to become self-aware and to discover your values and psychological needs. It also forces you to leave your comfort zone and conquer fear. There cannot be progress without suffering of some kind; it's the way of the world.

We cannot become fit without the struggle of exercise. We cannot become strong without the struggle of lifting weights. We cannot find love without being heartbroken and vulnerable. It is only after we have struggled, that our fears lessen and we can truly thrive.

Once you become fit, you are desensitised to the struggle of exercise. You can then become extremely fit. That doesn't mean that exercise is easy, but your threshold for pain has increased, meaning that it has less effect on you.

It's the same with love. When you have been vulnerable with a person and committed to them, you start to trust them a hundred percent. You can have a well-rounded, balanced relationship and let your love go to a deeper, more emotional state.

We can't become the person we want to be without conquering our fears. Fear is the struggle that holds people back more than money, more than status and more than education.

> *"Fear defeats more people than any one thing in the world."*
>
> — *Ralph Waldo Emmerson*

So many people live in fear. I'm not talking about people who live in war-torn countries, people in wealthy western societies live in fear too. People work at jobs they hate. They're afraid to leave, in case they end up skint. They're afraid of losing the social status that comes with having a job. They're afraid to live without the home comforts their salary has given them. Interestingly, if they take a step back in their careers or go part-time, they're less likely to be worried about what other people think.

Some middle-aged adults are still afraid of disappointing their parents with their life choices. Some people are afraid to be their real selves in case they aren't accepted by society or their loved ones. Fear is the wall that imprisons us.

However, the walls that define us and confine us are actually self-created. They can be destroyed only by yourself. This means that we are the only people who can conquer our own fears. People can help and support, but we are the only ones who can recognise, desensitise and destroy our own fears.

I was nervous about heights so I decided to face that fear by going skydiving. I was afraid of humiliation so I made myself sing at parties even though I knew I wasn't the best singer. I no longer have a fear of heights. I even go rock climbing from time to time. When I'm standing at the edge of The Cliffs of Moher, I'm still afraid of falling. However, I also remember the adrenaline rush of free falling from 10,000 feet with a parachute attached to my back.

Likewise, I'm not pursuing a singing career and I definitely don't have the X Factor but when I find myself at a sing-song at some house party, I can add to the atmosphere and sing along with the rest of them. I still fear ridicule but it doesn't stop me from taking action. That's the level I hope you will achieve.

My biggest fear was of water and I've been petrified of it since I was ten years old. In primary school, we had swimming lessons at school. It was my first real introduction to water because my family never really went swimming.

Although hesitant, I initially enjoyed being in the water. I did learn to swim and I suppose I was a bit more confident than my best friend James, who was very cautious.

Then disaster struck. On Easter Monday, 2005, my best friend James and his father drowned.

My world turned upside down. I cried non-stop for hours.

The newspaper article read:

> *Father and son (Michael and James) tragically died in a drowning accident in Co Clare. It is believed that James lost his footing on the edge of a small quarry while herding cattle with his father. Shortly after 6.30pm, James fell eight feet into the water below, and his father jumped in to try to save him.*

What wasn't mentioned was that Michael was unable to swim but he jumped in without hesitation to try to save his son. A true act of heroism and a most honourable way to die. I'm not very religious but this Bible verse comes to mind when I think of Michael's sacrifice for his son James:

> *"Greater love has no one than this: to lay down one's life for one's friends."*
>
> *– John 15:13*

In this case, Michael lay down his life for his son. Many parents are prepared to make the ultimate sacrifice for their children but few ever have to.

Through her grief and suffering, James' mother found comfort knowing that wherever her son was, her husband was taking care of him.

Apparently, James hit his head on the way down and was knocked unconscious, meaning that it was quick and he didn't suffer. I don't know if that was true, but I take solace, knowing that James was in his father's arms and wasn't alone in the end.

It's completely understandable therefore, that I was afraid of water. After all, it was responsible for the death of my friend and his father.

As the years went on, I did go into the water on occasion but I panicked the moment my head went under water. And I mean, panic. I thrashed about uncontrollably, my heart raced and a look of terror was written all over my face.

However, as time went on and I had started pursuing the goals on my bucket list, one of the opportunities that presented themselves to me was scuba diving.

Despite my panic underwater, I convinced myself that with the right equipment, I would be able to breathe and it would be fine.

When we were suited up, the instructor asked me to jump into the water from a pontoon. That was terrifying. I had never dived into water. Eventually, I jumped in. Embarrassingly, I panicked. Fortunately, with the help of my beloved partner, I regained my composure.

Again, I tried to go underwater. I was okay for a few seconds, but then the fear kicked in and I had to resurface. Eventually, the instructor kindly suggested that scuba diving wasn't for me.

I went back on land while my partner finished her lesson. This incident motivated me to finally tackle my fear of water.

Afterall, I was a grown adult and seventeen years older than the young boy I was when I lost my friend. I signed up for a block of eight swimming lessons. From my years of boxing, I knew I needed a good technical foundation so I went right back to the start with beginners' classes. I thought I'd be learning with a lot of small children, but actually I was the youngest in the class by about twenty years. There were a lot of older people wanting to learn how to swim. They had been advised to swim as part of their recovery for various injuries over the years.

Not being the oldest gave me some comfort. In addition, I chose a pool where my feet could touch the ground, even in the deep end. Both of these factors helped me to feel more confident about attending and yet, even with these comforts, I still panicked many times. However, I kept showing up. It was really difficult to struggle at something new again. As we get older, we tend to stay with pastimes that we're good at or feel we have a level of mastery over. We struggle to be 'new' at things again as we hate the feeling of being incompetent. We force children to try new things all the time, yet we rarely challenge ourselves. However, after four blocks of swimming lessons; a total of thirty-two lessons, I had conquered my fear of water. That summer, I jumped off the pier in Kilkee beach.

This was perhaps one of the biggest accomplishments on my bucket list. Perhaps it might not seem such a big accomplishment compared to some of the other feats I've achieved: amateur boxing, skydiving or running with bulls in Pamplona. However, with swimming, I had conquered my highest level of fear.

Fear is individualised; what one person fears, another may not. However, conquering your fear will give you an amazing sense of accomplishment. The accomplishments on your bucket list are also individualised. The tasks or experiences that you rate highly on your list will rarely be the highest for others. Just because I conquered my fear of water, it doesn't mean that water no longer scares me. It's just that fear doesn't stop me from jumping in anymore. My friend's death is no longer a justification to avoid any water-based activities and not to live my life to the full.

What is fear and how does it differ from anxiety?

Firstly, what exactly is fear?

What is anxiety?

Fear is an intrinsic human emotion designed to protect us from perceived threats by initiating the fight or flight response.

Anxiety is an intrinsic human feeling of apprehension, dread, agitation or discomfort.

The terms 'fear' and 'anxiety' are often used incorrectly and are not interchangeable. *Fear* is a negative emotional response to an ***immediate known*** threat.

Anxiety is a negative emotional response to a ***potential*** threat.

For example, you're walking down a dark alley by yourself and you feel *anxious* at the possibility someone might mug and rob you. This *may or may not* happen.

You're walking down a dark alley when someone pulls a gun on you. You are *fearful* for your life. The threat is immediate and you know exactly what it is: a person with a gun.

Take a moment to think about what is more prominent in your life: fear or anxiety?

Do you spend more time afraid of something that is going on right now or the potential of something happening in the future? We spend much more time being anxious about things that may or may not happen. The thought of fear is scarier than fear itself.

What happens when we become anxious or fearful?

When we perceive a situation to be a threat, the amygdala (the emotional regulator of the brain) is activated. It's important to note that sometimes the human brain doesn't differentiate between an immediate threat and a potential threat. The human brain also doesn't differentiate between a physical threat (such as a dog attack) and an emotional threat (such as a threat to your self-worth—for example, public speaking).

When the amygdala perceives a threat, it secretes a hormone which stimulates the adrenal gland. The adrenal gland secretes adrenaline (which is mainly the hormone cytosol). Adrenaline circulates through the body, causing an increase in heart rate, increase in blood flow and increase of oxygen and energy to the heart.

In other words, we can run faster, or fight for longer.

We either fight or flight.

This is a very basic description of the fight or flight response, but I think you get the picture. The problem is, in today's society, there are so many threats to self-worth:

- Not having enough money
- Not having the right job
- Not driving the right car
- Not being able to keep up with the Joneses

Our ancient brains can't differentiate between the above modern pressures and real, actual physical threats. Due to this, people are living anxious lives with high amounts of adrenaline running through their bodies. Studies have shown that this can have negative effects on our physical health such as heart attacks and strokes.

We are literally dying from stress, anxiety and fear.

Why do we need fear?

If fear and anxiety are so bad for us, then why do we need them?

As previously described, once a threat is perceived, they give us the fight or flight response. The release of adrenaline causes increased heart rate, muscle tension and increased alertness. These bodily changes, embedded in our fight-or-flight stress responses, are necessary for survival. Without this stress response, our mind wouldn't receive the alert of danger in enough time and our body wouldn't be able to prepare to fight or flight. As a result, the human race would have probably died out. However, fear has other qualities.

Both fear and anxiety can help to shape decisions in relation to survival. Fear is often based on past experiences, for example, a young child being bitten by a dog and later in life, being afraid of dogs. This happened to my partner. When she was riding a bike, a dog ran after her and bit her leg. There was no one around to help her and the dog chased her for a few hundred metres. She is now terrified of dogs. However, prior to the incident, she can remember really wanting a dog but her parents wouldn't get her one. Through experience, she has learned that some dogs can be dangerous and she has adjusted her behaviour accordingly in order to protect herself.

Fear can help to shape our decisions against behaviours that negatively impact our lives. For example, a young man overdoses on drugs, has a seizure and nearly dies. The fear of death is a catalyst for him to stop taking drugs. Fear can be very useful in changing behaviour that threatens the quality of our lives.

Fear is also necessary for the highest form of athletic and cognitive performance. All the top sports athletes are anxious or fearful to some degree when they perform to their best. They simply couldn't perform without it.

For example, you're playing a basketball game but you don't care whether you win or lose. As a result, you're not going to be alert and the adrenaline isn't flowing. Your mind isn't going to think quickly so you won't react quickly. However, your opponent has a controllable level of fear. His self-worth is under threat and he wants to win. His mind is going to fight, figuratively speaking. His influx of adrenaline will increase his breathing, making him react faster and think quicker. He will be able to perform at a much higher level than someone with no fear.

I was an amateur boxer, having won two All-Ireland medals and two international box cup medals. I like to have a bit of nervousness and anxiety going into a fight. I know it will make me sharp and take away any complacency. I know it will make me box better. As Rob Gilbert once said: "It's okay to have butterflies in your stomach, as long as you make them fly in formation."

This idea is confirmed by the Catastrophe model (Hardy et al., 1990). This model shows that if the athlete is confident in their ability to perform, as well as having high levels of somatic anxiety (anxious bodily sensations; sweaty palms, butterflies in the stomach, increased heart rate), they will be able to reach peak performance. However, when cognitive anxiety (negative thoughts) and somatic anxiety reaches a certain point, this has a catastrophic effect on performance.

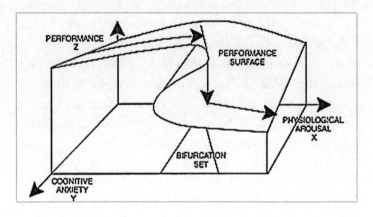

To perform best, whether that be in an exam, meeting, presentation or sports arena, you want to have medium-level somatic anxiety and low-level cognitive anxiety. If you're confident in your abilities, yet your body is nervous, you will perform well.

In relation to one's bucket list, the best way to become confident is to do the things we fear, consistently. Fear lessens when experience and capabilities increase. I'm not saying that if you're afraid of snakes, get a snake. However, putting yourself in controlled scenarios where you face your fears, will help you to desensitise yourself from them. It will also give you confidence when you tackle them again. It's like taking baby steps. Every previous success is proof that you can accomplish the next task.

For example, I hate snakes. They freak me out and I see very few advantages to them. However, when I'm at an event where I have an opportunity to hold one, I do. Why? Because it scares me. Every time I do it, it scares me less and less. I will never own one but I could tolerate someone who does. The most important thing is, I respect myself more every time I do it.

Therefore, it's a great idea to include on your bucket list: *'Conquer a fear'*.

If you can, don't do it just once; do it several times. The fear doesn't have to go away completely. Keep doing it until you gain confidence that if you have to face that particular fear one day, you can.

Fear is used as self-control

Another major benefit to having fear (or at least low-level fear), is that it provides the individual with a higher level of self-control. Fear of being fat gives you a higher level of control over your diet. Fear of failing a test gives you a higher level of control over your study plan and motivates you to study harder. Fear of being socially shamed can prevent anti-social behaviour such as theft, violence and even infidelity. Fear of being judged and humiliated can stop people from committing heinous acts.

Did you ever wonder what the world would be like if people didn't have any fear at all? At first

149

glance, we might think it would be positive. We could go skydiving. We could be who we want to be without fear of humiliation and ridicule. Low levels of fear are good but absolutely no fear is bad and a little scary as this story will show.

> *"Fear is a fundamental part of making good decisions."*
>
> *– (McGonigal, 2010)*

There was a case of a 24-year-old woman; let's call her Kate. Kate had developed a pattern of seizures following a very persistent fever. The seizures became more and more frequent and severe, even with medical intervention. Within a week, Kate's brain was in a state of nearly continuous seizure. It didn't look good. Due to the severity of the seizures, doctors were forced to perform emergency brain surgery to save her life and prevent permanent impairment. The surgery removed half of Kate's amygdala, the region in the brain that seemed to cause most of the seizures. The surgery was successful and the seizures drastically reduced in frequency and intensity.

However, all was not as it appeared to be. Several years later, Kate reappeared in the emergency room of the same hospital. She had suffered from another big seizure. The doctor who examined her described her as docile and distant, but medically sound. That's when things get very strange.

According to the original case report in the Journal of Neurology, Neurosurgery, and Psychiatry, Kate was left unattended for approximately 30 minutes. When the doctors returned, she was found in the room next to hers, performing oral sex on an elderly man.

You might surmise that after her brush with death, she was simply living life to the fullest. Perhaps he was a very charming old man. However, this behaviour probably wouldn't have even been believed in a soap opera. She would have gone for a hot young doctor and they probably wouldn't have been complete strangers.

Instead, she had gone for the old man next door who she didn't know. It appeared to be an act of opportunity rather than passion.

After further investigation, this wasn't the first time Kate had shown these behaviours. Kate continued to have seizures after the surgery. They usually occurred when she had forgotten to take her medication or over-applied herself.

For one or two hours after each seizure, she engaged in shocking sexual behaviours that weren't conducive to her normal personality. This included masturbating in public, sudden sexual advances and even trying to seduce family members. She also lost control of her food intake after the seizures, with her family reporting extreme binge-eating episodes.

What could explain this drastic and short-lived change in behaviour? What could turn a normal young woman into a calorie-crazed, sex-driven maniac who would engage in incest, given the chance? To discover this, they would have to look at what the surgeons did to Kate's brain during the surgery.

The surgery removed Kate's left amygdala. The amygdala, as previously mentioned, is the emotional regulator of the brain. The left side of the amygdala is a region of the brain associated with the detection and application of the fear response.

Kate's amygdala was essentially halved. The right side remained intact, which, for the most part, was enough for her to function normally without her left amygdala. However, her occasional seizures temporarily disabled her remaining amygdala which disarmed the detection of fear.

After every seizure, for a brief window in time, Kate had no functioning amygdala and was without fear.

Kate was not bound to any social constructs or morals fuelled by social conditioning. In this window, her behaviour became almost primal. She lost control over two of the most primal motivating forces in human behaviour: the need for food and the need for sex.

How does this bizarre medical case tie in with the personal development task of conquering fear?

Firstly, it helps us to see that we don't want to eradicate fear from our lives. We need small levels of fear—it is there for a reason.

Fear helps us to appraise and adjust behaviour that could be damaging to our health and well-being. It helps motivate positive behaviours. For example, fear of an early death would motivate an individual to work on their health and fitness. Fear enhances our ability for self-control and prevents us from readily succumbing to our primal needs and desires.

If you find yourself facing one of your fears (such as public speaking or performing in front of a large group of people) it might be reassuring to know that there will never be an absence of fear in those sorts of situations. You can never become desensitised to fear to the level that it's never there. The trick is to remember that you shouldn't strive for the absence of fear. When fear is present, it gives you the adrenaline to perform to the best of your ability.

For me, it was important to recognise that I didn't need an absence of fear, I just needed to reduce it by increasing my confidence. That insight made me feel closer to the person I wanted to be; someone who feels fear but isn't controlled by it.

The Dalai Lama said: "Fear does not prevent death, it prevents life." A certain amount of fear helps us to avoid life-threatening situations, but too much fear stops us from truly living. Fear prevents us from being our authentic selves, from striving to find our own self-proclaimed purpose in life. Conquer your fear by acknowledging that it will always be there.

How do we overcome anxiety?

Fear isn't as prevalent in our everyday lives because we don't often put ourselves in life-threatening situations. However, anxiety is much more common.

Remember, *fear* is the emotional response to an *immediate* threat, whereas *anxiety* is an emotional response to a *potential* threat.

The relationship between anxiety and the average person is summarised by the stoic philosopher Seneca:

"Our (anxieties) are more numerous than our dangers and we suffer more in imagination than reality."

To conquer fear, you need to control your anxiety. To control your anxiety, you need to avoid focusing on future events that might never happen. Instead, you need to focus on the present moment. Being able to focus on the present moment allows you to have control over your thoughts. By focusing on the here and now, it's impossible to worry about what could happen in the future. Mindfulness is the meditative technique of focusing the mind on the present moment.

To be mindful is to focus on the breath. Because the breath is a bodily function that occurs almost every second, it is a great anchor to the present. By focusing on your breath, you are linking your mind with your body and anchoring it to the present. This serves as a great technique that reduces anxiety by removing the focus from the future.

What is mindfulness?

Mindfulness is a meditation which is present-focused. You focus on being aware of what you're feeling in the present moment. This allows you to be free from self-judgement and over-analysis.

Mindfulness cannot be a goal. This is because goals are future based. With mindfulness, you have to be intentional with your time and focus paying attention to what's happening in the present moment.

There's no better way to bring yourself into the present moment than to focus on your breathing.

Because you're placing your awareness on what's happening right now, you are anchoring your thoughts to your body and the present moment. For most people, focusing on the breath is the best method of orienting themselves to the present. This isn't because the breath has some magical capability, but as long as you're alive, your breath is always with you.

If you don't believe me, try it. As you draw your next breath, focus on the rise of your stomach as you inhale, the feeling of the air through your nostrils and the expansion of your chest and then the fall of your stomach and chest on your exhale.

If you read the above and are aware of that feeling, then you're living in the moment.

As well as being aware of the breath, acknowledge how you are feeling. If you are sad, allow yourself to feel sad. If you are happy, allow yourself to feel happy. Do this without judgement. This is meditation at its most basic.

Numerous studies have shown that people who live in the moment are much happier. This is because anxious thoughts are usually about what happened in the past or what could happen in the future.

Most of the things that scare us are thoughts in our head.

What if this happens?

What if he says this?

What if they do not like me?

Most of what we fear hasn't happened.

Think about some of the things you have been afraid of:

- *Afraid of getting mugged?*
- *Afraid of travelling by yourself?*
- *Afraid of never finding a partner and dying alone?*

How many of your fears have actually come true? I'm guessing most of them didn't.

> *"I have known a great many troubles, but most of them never happened."*
>
> *– Mark Twain*

Catastrophizing is the process of thinking about bad things that *could* happen. Catastrophizing is a catalyst for depression and anxiety. Anxiety, by its very nature, means thinking about potential negative outcomes in the future. If you hoist yourself into awareness of the present moment, the anxiety declines. Additionally, focusing on your breathing reduces focus on anxious body cues (sweaty palms and butterflies in the stomach). This is also known as 'somatic anxiety', or commonly called 'body anxiety'.

By meditating and focusing on the breath, you will lower your levels of body anxiety. By lowering your anxiety, you are increasing your health. Mindfulness reduces stress, boosts immune functioning, reduces chronic pain, decreases blood pressure, and helps patients cope with cancer. It can even lower the risk of heart disease.

Another benefit to mindfulness is that it blurs the line between self and others. When people are present, they're more likely to be aware of the people around them. They can be more perceptive to other people's wants and needs.

When someone is anxious and fearful, the constant focus is on themselves, not others.

People who are present have the capacity to notice other people and to see themselves as part of humanity. Highly mindful people, such as monks, talk about being "one with everything".

People who are more mindful of others tend to be happier. When you worry about someone else, your own problems fade away. When you are grateful for other people, your perception of life changes. You become a much more caring and happier person.

Not only do mindful people have higher levels of happiness, they tend to have higher levels of self-esteem. If a mindful person is on the receiving end of criticism, they can be more resilient. They don't feel like the criticism is an attack on their self-worth. Mindfulness almost sounds like a superpower!

Mindfulness, practised consistently over a few months, can result in a more resilient and well-rounded person. Mindfulness, practised over a lifetime, can result in a caring, modest person who is resilient and unshakeable; someone with an air about them who is worthy of admiration.

Have you ever met someone like that?

I have; my grandmother. There is something special about my grandmother and everyone else agrees. She has an air about her; almost a spiritual vibe. This aura comes from the fact that my grandmother puts everyone above herself.

It's almost like she exists to serve people. She is compassionate, kind, caring and considerate. She refuses to take compliments. If you try to compliment her, she attributes the achievement to someone else. She never worries about her own life; she only worries about others. Her focus is on other people. As a result, she has the ability to be grateful for everything.

She has seven children, all of whom have the highest respect and admiration for her. They rarely talk to each other due to hectic schedules, but each one of them stays in contact with her regularly. I hope to have half the admiration from my children that my grandmother has from hers.

I often wondered how she turned out the way she did. Then I discovered that her own mother died when she was very young. Being the eldest child, my grandmother took on a mothering role in her early teens. She also became a nurse and served people throughout her entire career. My grandmother was a devout Christian, went to mass every single day and visited religious pilgrimage sites on many occasions. She has been to Medjugorje at least ten times.

Most of all, my grandmother prays, reflects and is grateful for an hour a day. This happens every day, whether she's sick or tired, whether there's a wedding or funeral. She gets up early and prays, spending 90% of that time praying for others.

It's not the fact that she's a Christian and prays that is admirable. It's the fact that she sets aside time for self-reflection, gratitude and focusing on others. She's intentional with her time and has a personal development routine.

We can all achieve this by setting aside time each day for reflection, mindfulness and gratitude. There are a lot of meditation apps geared towards 5 or 10 minutes of simple meditation. However, at least half an hour each day is needed to make a difference.

I'm not saying: "Don't bother trying ten minutes." Heck no! I'm saying: try to build up to half an hour. Try to make that your consistent dedicated time.

Most people will say: "I don't have half an hour."

If you don't have half an hour, you don't have a life.

Realistically, you probably don't want to sacrifice time allocated for something you've defined as essential, but you know deep down, it isn't. For example, staying up late to watch TV. Anyone can get up half an hour earlier to practise mindfulness, gratitude and affirmations. For as long as you continue to practise, it will change your life. As with your body, if you do weights, you become strong. Once you stop, your muscles decrease and become weaker. The same goes with self-improvement. It's a lifestyle, not just a regime.

If you set aside that time for devotion, you could be like my grandmother. A normal, average woman, who touches everyone she meets and is worshipped like royalty by the people in her inner circle.

Life hacks

In conjunction with mindfulness, gratitude and affirmations, there are a few life hacks to help you become happier. The first of these is the realisation that **"Your thoughts are not facts"**. Sometimes, people punish themselves for their thoughts. Perhaps they feel jealous of a friend's success, or think that a colleague's baby is ugly. When people have thoughts like these, they can become disappointed, or even disgusted, in themselves. They start self-deprecating and bashing themselves up internally. In turn, this makes them feel even worse about themselves and they start to believe they don't deserve happiness. This feeling shapes their actions, perhaps making them miss out on opportunities they could enjoy.

This cycle can be explained with basic Cognitive behavioural therapy. Cognitive Behavioural Therapy (or CBT) is based on the prowess that thoughts, emotions and behaviours are interconnected. Negative thoughts and emotions can cause a vicious cycle of negative behaviours, that in turn, lead to further negative thoughts.

CBT helps to overcome negative thinking by breaking thoughts down into smaller parts. Negative thoughts are replaced with positive thoughts. Behaviour is altered to match the new positive thoughts. This leads to positive emotions that then lead to more positive thoughts.

This is achieved by realising that *thoughts are not facts.*

Perhaps your boss shouts at you or is unpleasant to you. Perhaps thoughts swirl around your mind about the numerous ways he could die. This does not make you a murderer, an accomplice or even a bad person. As a matter of fact, it doesn't even mean you want your boss dead.

Simply, your emotions of anger and sadness are causing your thoughts to exaggerate.

The thought about your boss dying is not a fact. It doesn't mean he *will* die. Thoughts come from nowhere and they aren't a direct reflection of your morals. Thoughts just arrive in our heads.

They could come from our confused subconscious or they could com e from our environment, experiences, relationships or desires. They're a mixture of everything and are greatly linked to our emotions. However, they mean nothing unless you put them into action.

Negative emotions are related to your physical senses. For example, when hungover, the body feels poorly, physically. The body then tries to find thoughts that justify this poor feeling. It forces us to look at the conversations we had while drunk, trying to find anything that we could have said or done to insult someone. This is the mind looking for justification for the body feeling bad.

In Ireland, this is called *"The Fear"*.

The term describes the anxiety induced by drink and the process by which the mind finds thoughts to justify it.

I believe that people who can train their minds to blame the alcohol for the feeling (and not themselves) have the least anxious hangovers. In most cases, it's the negative thoughts that cause more inner turmoil than the physical effects of alcohol.

You can have a negative thought, yet not be a negative person. The trick is not to verbalise or act on your thoughts.

Changing your thought to a positive (or even neutral) one could positively change the way you feel and act.

For example, "I'm not good at giving presentations at work" is a negative thought that will make you feel anxious beforehand. It will most likely result in you behaving anxiously, fidgeting and maybe even stumbling over your words. In turn, that would just reconfirm your negative thoughts.

Instead, if you change that thought to a more positive one such as: "I have far more experience giving presentations now and I have learned from my past mistakes."

If you say this to yourself a few dozen times, you will feel more relaxed. You'll have more confidence and less nerves.

As we've discussed before, you will still feel nervous but the adrenaline will help you to perform. You need that bit of fear to perform at your best. You don't want your fear to disappear completely as that would mean you don't care about the outcome at all.

This use of basic CBT, ("thoughts are not facts") and reaching for more positive thoughts works amazingly well with mindfulness. Most of our negative thoughts are related to anxiety and are anticipations of potentially damaging future events. Mindfulness reduces body anxiety and keeps people in the present. The approach of: "Thoughts are not facts" will help you to overcome particularly difficult thoughts.

Another life hack that works alongside mindfulness is the realisation that most people are self-absorbed and are not focused on you.

I don't mean that people don't care about you or that you shouldn't care about yourself. What I'm saying is, most people are so absorbed by their own struggles and insecurities, that they aren't focused on yours.

When you're on the dance floor with your partner, there's no need to think that everyone is laughing at you. Most people are too busy thinking about their own insecurities. Yes, they might notice that you're not the greatest dancer. They might even mention it to you as a joke, but it's only an observation. They're too wrapped up in their own concerns to think twice about your dancing.

Most people, faced with that jokey comment, will take it as detrimental to their self-worth. If the observer grades the dancing as "negativity: 1", the receiver assumes it's a grading of negativity: 9". They then stop any action that warranted the comment. There's simply no need to take the comment so hard.

Remove the audience and stay at the surface.

There is no audience waiting to notice your faults. A throwaway joking comment about your performance is not a judgement of your self-worth. To improve your performance, stop thinking about perceived criticisms and stop imagining what others think. More than likely, they are not thinking about you.

By having this mindset, you have the ability to be mindful. When you try something new, you'll be able to stay in the present moment. You will enjoy it and concentrate on improving your skill rather than worrying about ridicule.

I have used this technique of 'removing the audience' with a number of young people who experience social anxiety.

I spoke with a young person who wouldn't leave their village or venture outside to another village. She believed that if she went somewhere new, everyone would be staring at her. We discussed this in depth.

I asked: "When you're in your hometown where you feel comfortable, do you stare at people you don't know?"

She replied: "Obviously not."

"Why would strangers stare at you when you're in their town?" I ventured. "What is so special about you that everyone has to stare at you?"

"They won't." With her reply came the realisation. It's easy to become anxious and self-absorbed. We believe our actions have a higher onus on others and it's just not the case. Most of the time, people do not care about others. It would be great if they did, but they don't. It is liberating to realise that you're not so special for people to care about the trivial things you do in your life.

'Removing the audience' allows you to be more present, which ties in with our next life hack: 'Savouring'.

'Savouring' is being in the moment and enjoying the daily pleasures of life as they come. It is removing oneself from the future or the past. It is simply being and doing with appreciation.

For example, have you ever gone to a new restaurant and as soon as you get there, you think: "I would like to come back here again." Before you've even savoured the current experience, you're already projecting into the future. Before you think ahead, try to truly experience the present. That is where life is lived and best experienced.

This is depicted well in the book "Eat, Pray, Love". In her memoirs, Elizabeth Gilbert writes about a friend who sees a beautiful place and immediately says "It's so beautiful here! I want to come back here someday!"

> "It takes all (my) persuasive powers," writes Gilbert, "to try to convince her that she is already here."

Be in the moment. **Savour it.**

It's helpful to stay in the moment if you use your senses:

- **Smell:** *What can you smell? Does it smell good?*
- **Sight:** *How amazing is the view?*
- **Touch:** *What is the texture of the cup in your hands?*
- **Taste:** *How good does that beer taste?*
- **Sound:** *What can you hear? Is it a pleasant sound?*

I have learned to cherish the good moments in life, even the day-to-day things like enjoying a cup of tea when I come home from work. It makes me feel so relaxed and it's a daily pleasure I get to enjoy day in, day out.

The benefits of 'Savouring' are even supported by research. Studies have shown that participants who took a few minutes each day to actively savour something, started to experience higher levels of happiness. Simple activities they might have hurried, such as quickly downing a cup of tea, gave them much more positive emotions when savoured slowly.

Mindfulness Reduces Aggression

How does 'being in the moment' make someone less aggressive?

Practising mindfulness enables you to be more present in the moment, which in turn, lessens self-absorption and ego.

Mindful individuals are less likely to allow comments from 'the audience' to affect their self-worth and self-esteem. They are more likely to take things at the surface level.

Additionally, practising mindfulness for oneself, gives the ability to be more mindful of others. As a result, it can help to create a feeling of connection with other people.

To quote a common phrase of monks:

> *"Mindfulness makes you at one with the universe."*

Therefore, mindfulness reduces anger by removing self-absorption and creating a feeling of connection to others. It increases the ability to take negative comments at surface level which also reduces anger. It increases the distance between the emotional response and the action. It prevents you from reacting to a trigger which would normally anger you.

Mindfulness allows you to recognize the spark before it becomes a flame.

Focusing on the present reboots your mind so you can respond thoughtfully rather than automatically. Instead of firing back in anger or closing down automatically in fear, mindfulness provides a small window to pause and change how you'll respond.

Mindfulness, if practised consistently, gives the individual the chance to say to themselves, "This is about to happen, am I okay with that?" An individual who can do this has higher levels of self-control.

Acceptance

Every person that has ever walked the earth has experienced various levels of suffering.

Whether it's an ex that broke your heart, friends that let you down or financial struggles, we have all experienced pain. There are certain problems that need to be addressed immediately—for example, hunger and shelter. These are Level One physiological needs on Maslow's hierarchy of needs.

However, there are other sufferings which are simply daily irritations; rush-hour traffic, poor Wi-Fi connection, your partner forgetting to buy your favourite coffee. If we allow it, such minor sufferings can prevent us from enjoying life. The human brain is designed to avoid suffering when possible, avoiding negative thoughts, feelings and emotions.

This is why negative feelings surface when these daily irritations occur. However, negative feelings and daily irritations can't be avoided. By trying to resist them, we're only magnifying their pain. By actively trying to avoid them, we're giving them power over our emotions.

We don't need to do this.

What is the remedy to this? **Acceptance:** Accepting there will always be daily irritations and daily suffering.

It's useful to accept the particular irritations you are prone to. Once you have established the irritations which can bother you, it's important to face those irritations and accept them as they are.

Rather than actively avoid them, it's more beneficial to resist trying to manipulate or change them.

Mindfulness allows you to be in the present moment.

Trying to change or manipulate daily irritations only leads to frustration and fatigue. Acceptance relieves you from this. This becomes apparent in people who have accepted a daily irritation that they find challenging.

For example, I live fifteen minutes away from my office. If I had to travel for an hour to get to work, I would find it deeply frustrating. However, I know a lot of people who live in remote locations who travel at least an hour to get to work. They have accepted it as a way of life. They don't suffer. They stick on a podcast or audiobook and use the time to unwind after work. They accept it as their way of life.

That is how we should view our daily irritations.

I'm not saying we have to just lie down and accept bad behaviour or every negative event in life. Acceptance doesn't mean you have to like what's happening.

What I'm saying is: if there's a circumstance that bothers you, then change it! If you can't change it, then strive to accept it.

My friend drives one hour to get to work. She loves her job so she accepts the commute. However, if she didn't like her job, she would have looked for something closer. By accepting the need for her commute, she is preventing herself from being irritated or miserable.

Take a look at your own lifestyle:

- What are your daily irritations?

- Can you change them?

- If not, can you strive to accept them?

Seeing the new in the old

Have you ever had the experience of driving home along a familiar route, only to realise that you've been driving on auto-pilot? You expect a familiar landmark to remind you that you're nearly home, only to realise you must have passed it five minutes ago! It has happened to me on several occasions. I could have been thinking about work, processing all that had happened that day, when I suddenly realise, I'm not in the present moment!

These autopilot moments happen when we're lost in our thoughts. We're usually projecting into the future or ruminating over events in the past. We aren't aware of our present experience.

As a result, life passes us by.

The best way to prevent these time blackouts is to develop the habit of always seeing the new in the old. When doing repetitive or monotonous tasks, such as driving home, try to look for the new in the familiar journey. This can be anything from memorising every exit, observing what's going on at the side of the road or even looking for coloured registration plates. This doesn't only apply to driving; you can do this while going out for a walk or when cutting the grass. Try to be on the look-out for a beautiful flower or a cool-shaped stone. Analyse it as though it's the first time you've ever seen it.

This process creates awareness of the present moment and has several different benefits. It helps you to focus on the here and now, as well as helping you to renew the love for something you already had. It is similar to a small boy going to the park for the first time; how awestruck he is! He is observing new things all the time. We can tap into that feeling of excitement again; by observing anew. As a result, life doesn't simply pass us by.

In summary, the following life hacks are important strategies that we can incorporate into our lifestyles:

- Your thoughts are not facts
- Remove the audience and stay at the surface
- Reduce aggression levels
- Acceptance
- See the new in the old

These lessons can be applied to everyday life and will help you to become a more emotionally balanced person. They are most effective when used alongside mindfulness. The pair provides a dual system:

- Mindfulness calms the body
- The hacks calm the mind

We have discussed many physical and personal benefits of mindfulness. However, without intentionality, there are little results. It's the same as watching an inspiring travel video and saying to yourself "I will go there one day." By not being intentional about your plans, you never end up going.

"A goal without action is just a dream."

Put your plan in action. Implement mindfulness into your day-to-day routine. This consistently takes effort, but mindfulness itself is easy. It is identifying where you are and how you are feeling at this very moment. It is not about trying to improve yourself or get anywhere. It is simply about being yourself in the present moment.

We need more flow in our life

Mindfulness brings us to a heightened state of both physical and self-actualised performance. However, there is no higher state of psychological performance than **flow.**

Flow is a psychological state that emerges when an individual achieves a balance between the challenges of a task's demands and their own skill level (which allows them to meet these demands).

Flow mainly consists of the harmony between demands and skill. More specifically, flow occurs when the consciousness of the person is fully immersed in the completion of a task. Flow occurs when:

- The mind is goal-directed
- The person perceives their skills as capable of meeting the demands of the goal.

When a person is 'in flow', they become en-grossed in their performance. They experience intrinsic rewarding feelings, which are then accompanied by success and higher performance. This was described by Csikszentmihalyi in 1990:

> *"The balance between demand and skill is the contributing factor to the characteristics of flow which are the action-awareness merging, narrowing of attention, internal locus of control, loss of self-consciousness, a transformation of time and greater intrinsic satisfaction."*

Nine characteristics of the flow experience arose from the extensive research of: Cikszentmihalyi, 1990, Voelk & Morris, 1994, Jackson & Marsh, 1996 and Boniface, 2000.

The **nine characteristics scale** has been found to be consistently linear across categorical variables such as: age, gender, ethnicity, and socioeconomic class. It has proven to stand the test of time as it is still used in modern research today.

1. Skill-challenge balance

The first of the nine characteristics is the "Skill-challenge balance". This represents how the individual feels when there is a balance between the task demands and their capabilities.

2. Action-awareness merging

"Action-awareness merging" is the lack of awareness of the self, as separate from the actions being performed. The person is engrossed with the task being performed.

3. Clear goals

"Clear goals" occur when goals are clearly defined and are understood by the individual performing the task.

4. Unambiguous feedback

"Unambiguous feedback" occurs when there is direct and instant feedback given in regard to performance and goal progression.

5. Concentration on the task at hand

"Concentration on the task at hand" is the narrowing of focus to the stimuli that are related to the task.

6. Sense of control

"Sense of control" is exercising a sense of control without fully being in control.

7. Loss of self-consciousness

"Loss of self-consciousness" occurs when the awareness of the self disappears and the individual becomes one with the activity.

8. Transformation of time

"Transformation of time" is the loss of awareness of time.

9. Autotelic experience

Finally, "Autotelic experience" is an intrinsically rewarding experience accompanied by positive emotions. An example: perhaps you are playing a sport or an instrument (or maybe even doing a presentation). You are nervous, but you feel you have the skills to get the job done. You go in there and absolutely 'nail it'! Time flies. You're there for half an hour but it feels like only five minutes. You come out, buzzing with excitement. When you reflect back, you remember how focused you were. Nothing seemed to distract you. *That is flow.* Flow is that state of narrow focus when doing something you enjoy and you're good at.

For flow to occur, the activity that the individual is performing should be self-justifying and intrinsically rewarding. The individual must enjoy the activity thoroughly. The purpose of the activity should be individual enjoyment, rather than external rewards (such as recognition from others).

Persistence is another contributor to flow. Research has discovered a relationship between the flow state and consistency in activity participation. We usually experience flow when we have spent a considerable amount of time practising and honing our skills in that activity. Therefore, the more often someone performs a desirable task, the more likely they will experience flow. Similarly, the more often someone performs a desirable task, the better they will become at self-engaging into the flow experience.

Another significant contributor to flow is **Goal Clarification.**

Flow occurs when an individual establishes a clear-cut set of goals requiring skilled performance. When there is a clear goal, it provides the individual with a focus for their concentration. It allows them to develop feelings of control and provides a means to become in tune with one's performance.

Flow is a psychological state. Like any state of mind, it can be influenced by multiple factors. How one person experiences flow can be different to another.

Flow is the state we enter when we are doing something we are good at and something we enjoy.

• When was the last time you experienced flow?

- During that activity, how long were you actually in flow?

In our modern generation, we don't always experience flow in our activities. At times, we can plod through our work with indifference rather than fully immersing ourselves in the activity at hand. As a result, we lose out on experiencing the state of flow and the feeling of reward from the activity we have just completed.

You can achieve flow from doing even the most menial tasks, such as sweeping the floor and washing the dishes. Flow can be achieved by aiming to do a good job, regardless of the type of work.

I'm not saying that flow can occur for everyone, doing every activity. That would take a high level of self-actualisation and enlightenment. However, perhaps there is a task that you don't mind doing. You can turn that indifference into an intrinsically rewarding activity. There are numerous benefits to entering a state of flow regularly.

When people develop higher levels of flow, they gain higher levels of emotional stability and happiness. People who experience a flow state have the ability to enjoy the activity significantly more; it becomes much more fulfilling. Research shows that being in a flow state is linked to increased levels of happiness and self-actualization. In contrast, people who aren't in flow state experience negative emotions such as fear and anxiety. Flow and happiness act as a buffer against that fear. Flow helps to increase resilience.

For these reasons (and many more), try to include activities in your bucket list that enable you to experience flow. For me, that includes playing sports or boxing. For you, it might mean a dance class or 5-a-side soccer. You might tell yourself that you don't have enough time for these hobbies. However, you'll reap the rewards when you experience the feeling of flow you achieve from these past-times. It will far outweigh having a busy schedule for one day during the week.

9 characteristics of flow:
- Challenge skill balance
- Action-awareness merging
- Clear goals
- Unambiguous feedback
- Concentration on the task at hand
- Paradox of control
- Loss of self-consciousness
- Transformation of time
- Autotelic experience

Write down the tasks that you experience flow in.

Number them in order of preference and practicality.

Try to implement at least one of these tasks into your weekly life.

1. _____

2. _____

3. _____

4. _____

5. _____

CHAPTER TEN

Finances

IT'S IMPOSSIBLE TO COMPLETE a bucket list without taking financial awareness into consideration.

You might ask why a book about bucket lists would need to include a chapter about finance. It's a good question.

The reason is, if you don't have adequate control of your finances, it will be very difficult to pursue your bucket list. If you spend your time working two jobs or worrying about how to pay the bills, it will be difficult to plan ahead. It will be near impossible to travel and have great experiences that force you out of your comfort zone if you can't even afford to leave work for a week.

Finances are one of the most common worries people have. It's also the biggest contributing factor to marriage difficulty. A survey carried out by Capital One showed that:

- 77% of Americans feel anxious about their finances.

- 58% of Americans feel that finances control their lives.
- 52% have difficulty controlling their finance-related anxieties.

Worries about their financial future include:

- not having enough money to retire.
- keeping up with the cost of living.
- managing debt levels.

That's a large amount of the population constantly worrying about finances. Of course, this isn't just in America; many people around the world worry about finance. For this reason, I feel that financial awareness and financial knowledge is worthy of featuring on any bucket list.

Before we begin, a disclaimer: I am not a financial advisor!

I have no qualifications in finance and I am not rich.

I purchased two houses in my mid-to-late twenties, but that's it. However, since acquiring these properties, I have been able to spend six months abroad, take three trips around Europe and a road trip around America. All of this, by the time I was twenty-seven. I didn't accumulate any debt except for my mortgages which are, of course, investments. One of my houses is a rental so that debt is paid by my tenants.

Therefore, I have acquired some financial knowledge and I've discovered small financial tricks that work. I also know how to travel on a budget, which we will discuss in detail later.

My journey of financial discovery began when I studied a semester abroad at a University in Canada. For six months, I was an undergrad at Wilfrid Laurier University in Waterloo, Ontario.

At only nineteen years old, I worked like a slave to pay for this semester abroad. During my first and second year of University in Ireland, I worked part-time. Due to University fees in Ireland being relatively low, I was able to stash a decent amount of cash away.

For my third year, I set off to Canada with one other girl in my class. She had taken out a €10k loan to fund her trip. When we arrived and met the other exchange students, we quickly realised we were the only two students whose parents hadn't paid for their trip.

That made me think. What did their parents work at? What did they do that made them wealthy enough? How could they afford to pay for their child's accommodation, food, trips and drinking for six months? It started me thinking about finances.

When I finished college and got my first job, I discovered that my friend had traded in his €13k car. He paid a €5k deposit towards a €30k+ car. His monthly payments were then €400.

I felt this wasn't a wise decision. I started to read lots of books about finances. My interest in reading these types of books (and the time I put into it) was probably magnified during the lockdown surrounding the Coronavirus.

I then made the decision to invest a similar amount than my friend had spent on his car. However, I invested the money into a rental property instead. It was that first decisive move. I took a risk for a better financial future. Compared to young adults my age, I went against the grain. It changed me as a person and I've never looked back since.

Since then, I have been seeking ways to increase my financial stability and build up passive forms of income. Personally, I believe this has allowed me to become a better person. Why? Because I'm not worried anymore about trying to keep up with the Joneses. Unfortunately, the Joneses will have to work well into their sixties before they can retire. I won't.

I don't feel the need to stay in a high-paying job I hate. I know the benefits of living within my means. I don't buy more than I need and I have a minimalist financial perspective.

The first book I would recommend to any reader who wants to start their financial journey is "The Richest Man in Babylon" by George S. Clason. It's a simplistic personal finance book conveyed through an ancient fictional tale. It explains 'The Seven Cures to a Lean Purse' (financial stability) and 'The Five Rules of Gold' (Financial Growth). These rules are simple, but they really do work. This book is renowned across the globe as a great financial guide. It's recognised especially as an ideal financial starter book.

Let's take a look at the 'Seven Cures to a Lean Purse', otherwise known as 'The seven rules to financial stability'.

The Seven Cures to a Lean Purse

1. **Start thy purse to fattening:** or in modern terms: **"how to build savings".** It is based on the principle of "Paying yourself first". Paying yourself first means that you should save money before you pay for anything. Most people only save what is left at the end of the month after their bills and leisure activities. Some months, they save quite a bit; other months, they don't save anything at all. By

paying yourself first, you assign an amount to put into savings or investments as soon as you get paid. The remaining is allocated for bills and leisure activities. By saving or investing an assigned amount each month, you can watch your savings grow.

2. **Control thy expenditures**—in other words: **Don't spend every penny you make.** Otherwise, no matter how high your income becomes, you will always be broke. A lot of people live paycheck to paycheck. Whatever they earn, they spend. They think that if they get a pay rise, their problems will be over. For the first few months, they are. However, gradually, they increase their spending to match their new wages. Despite the increase in earnings, they continue to live paycheck to paycheck, spending every penny they make. This is called 'life inflation'. Many people with financially rewarding jobs succumb to this. You must control your expenditure. This involves budgeting and allocating a designated amount on leisure activities.

3. **Make thy gold multiply.** In modern terms, this means: **'make your money work for you'.** Putting money into a savings account is great. It provides you with a great sense of security should any unforeseen circumstances arise (such as the loss of a job, car breakdown etc). However, having an amount of money in a savings account actually loses its buying pow-

er over time. This is due to inflation; the increase in price of everyday items. Over time, inflation causes your buying power to diminish. For example, let's say you have £10k in a savings account right now. In ten years' time, you'd be able to buy much less than what you can buy today. We've all heard the familiar lament from our grandparents: "Everything was cheaper in my day!" And they were right. Make your money work for you by investing in assets that will increase in value, for example: index funds, mutual funds, property or gold and silver. Of course, the value of these can fluctuate, but over a long period of time, their value increases. Invest in assets that appreciate or stocks with compound interest.

4. **Guard thy treasures from loss.** Your number one priority is to **keep your investment safe** from loss. Make sure that you only invest in schemes you understand. Don't give your money to someone else to invest for you. You are the shepherd of your own financial flock. A safe investment that increases over time is better than a risky investment that promises to get rich quick. Get-rich-quick schemes don't work. Instead of making you rich, they will more likely bleed you dry. Remember: "If it sounds too good to be true, it usually is." Play the long game with investments.

5. **Make of thy dwelling a profitable investment.** There are times when renting is better.

However, over a lifespan, it's much more beneficial to have **bought your own home and paid off all your mortgage.** Otherwise, when renting, you're simply pumping that money into someone else's pocket. If you can, aim to buy your own house rather than renting for the rest of your life.

6. **Ensure a future income.** In order to ensure a future income, it is wise to try to create passive forms of income. Income can be generated passively in areas such as: rental properties, pensions, index funds and dividends. You won't be able to work forever, so it's important to try to create income streams that can sustain you in retirement. It's sensible to try to diversify your incomes, rather than just relying on one (such as a pension). Aim to have multiple streams of income so that if something happens to one of them, you have the others to sustain you.

7. **Increase thy ability to earn.** You can grow your earning power by various different means. Perhaps you can go back to education so that you can work for a higher salary. Perhaps you could build your skills or gain work experience in a certain field. Maybe you could even go for that promotion and take on higher levels of responsibility. The more money you can acquire, the more you can put into your investments. The more wealth you acquire, the more sustainable your life becomes.

If followed, the above seven rules can prevent people from living beyond their means, sliding into debt and squandering their money. It will encourage them to budget, invest some of their income and plan for tomorrow. It is very solid advice.

Let's look at some more financial rules in relation to investing, taken from "The Richest Man in Babylon". The below '5 Rules of Gold' go into even more detail about generating wealth. They also warn against the common pitfalls of investing.

1. **Gold cometh gladly and in increasing quantity to any man who will put by, not less than one-tenth of his earnings, to create an estate for his future and that of his family.** Or in modern parlance: *"Money comes to those who save."* It's a good idea to save 10% of your income. You should then convert it to investment capital. Rule 1 of financial advice states: you should pay yourself first. The suggested amount is 10%. However, in the current climate, I would suggest that this figure is a bit low. My recommendation would be that 15% would be a much better amount to aim for. By investing 15% into passive income streams, it will help greatly to prepare for the future.

2. **Gold laboreth diligently and contentedly for the wise owner who finds for it profitable employment, multiplying even as the flocks of the field.** It is wise to *invest your money in schemes which will enable it to grow and multiply.* You can make use of compound interest which will allow your money to grow. Compound interest is when you earn money back on the money you've invested. You then earn more interest on the money you have invested. Add that to the interest you've made in the first year, and it grows year after year.

3. **Gold clingeth to the protection of the cautious owner who invests it under the advice of men wise in its handling.** *Don't take advice from someone who doesn't have the experience.* Find a successful model to copy when it comes to investing your money. Invest in schemes you understand and with people who are knowledgeable in the area. I have a friend who waxes lyrical about bitcoin and how profitable it is. However, he doesn't invest in bitcoin himself, so I don't take the advice on board. Only take advice from the experts; people who practise what they preach. Invest cautiously. Get rich quick schemes rarely work. Wealth is usually acquired slowly and cautiously.

4. **Gold slippeth away from the man who invests it in businesses or purposes with which he is not familiar or which are not approved by those skilled in its keep.** *Invest in what you know.* Don't put money in something you don't fully understand. People can accumulate wealth from a number of avenues. However, just because you see someone accumulate wealth in a certain way, that doesn't mean it's the best way for you. My friend owns an equestrian centre. He has bought and sold horses, making €10-15k profits at times. Needless to say, I don't invest in horses because I don't have his background or expertise in horses. Meanwhile, unlike me, he doesn't invest in stocks. We both invest, but not in things we don't understand.

5. **Gold flees the man who would force it to impossible earnings or who followeth the alluring advice of tricksters and schemers or who trusts it to his own inexperience and romantic desires in investment.** The fastest way to go broke is to try to get rich quickly. We all hear rumours about how someone became a millionaire overnight. However, far more people have lost wealth by trying to accumulate it quickly or by listening to cons. Wealth does not come quickly. It comes from diligence, patience and delaying the wants of today for the needs of tomorrow. Do not try to get rich quick.

The above rules, if followed, will allow you to become wealthy over time. However, they may not make you rich and there is a difference. Most people do not distinguish the difference between being rich and being wealthy. Being rich is having a considerably large amount of money. Being wealthy is defined by the length of time you are able to sustain your life by your investments, without having to work. A good metaphor that I use when distinguishing the two is:

> *Being rich is like having two water trucks in the desert.*
>
> *You have far more than you need but once they are gone, they are gone.*

Being wealthy, however, is like having a few wells in the desert. Some may be dry at times and others will be full, but you should have constant access to water, no matter what. The aim is to be wealthy, not rich.

Be aware of the difference. I think that being financially aware should be on everyone's bucket list. Knowing how to become wealthy and how to avoid common financial pitfalls should be a common goal. Simply stated:

> *"happen to your money and don't just let your money happen to you"*.

Know where your money goes and what it's spent on. On your bucket list, be intentional with your money, not just your travel.

The above is a very brief summarisation of the financial rules from 'The Richest Man in Babylon'. Reading it can lead to great financial awareness. I recommend that everyone put this task on their bucket list. I would also recommend that this be one of the tasks you strive to complete early on. It will make everything else easier for you, once you have your finances under control.

For me, however, it didn't simply stop at financial awareness. Awareness was half of the problem solved. I needed to solve the other half. The other half of my financial goal is financial independence. Financial independence, as outlined by Wikipedia, is the status obtained by having enough income to pay one's expenditure for the rest of one's life without having to be employed or dependent on others. Income earned, without having to work at a job, is commonly referred to as 'passive income'. Financial independence is having enough passive income streams to sustain your lifestyle.

Passive income doesn't mean you do nothing. There is some effort and time involved, but it's not as intensive, nor as timely as a full-time job.

The movement to achieve this is called **F.I.R.E.** Even though it is not a household phrase, it is used worldwide.

F.I.R.E. stands for:

"**F**inancial **I**ndependence, **R**etire **E**arly."

The F.I.R.E movement focuses on financial independence. It is based on the premise that, with enough money, you no longer have to work. You have freedom of choice with how you spend your time. To achieve this, **F.I.R.E.** movement adherents cut down on their expenses while finding ways to increase their current income. That could involve smart investing or starting new ventures that generate extra cash.

For those in the F.I.R.E. movement, "financial independence" doesn't mean just sitting on some tropical beach or playing golf all the time. It means reaching the point where you don't have to work a full-time job if you don't want to. You can scale back to a part-time job or simply stop working altogether. The choice is yours and that is the true driving force for me. I do not want to be rich or famous or have an extravagant life. I simply want to have the freedom to choose how I would like to spend my time. If my kids had a football match, I would like to be able to attend. If a family member needed help, I would like to have the availability to help them. If I see an amazing location on TV that I'd want to travel to, I want to be able to jump on a plane and do that. For me, I will give up fancy dinners, nice cars and 5-star hotels for my freedom. A job is such a normalised part of life and we know why we need it. We need money to buy food and to pay for the roof over our heads, but we have forgotten at what expense. A full-time job means giving up your day, your freedom and often your passions. Most people don't break their day down and realise what little free time they actually have.

We should be getting 8 hours of sleep. For those 8 hours, we're either sleeping, in bed trying to sleep, reading a book to wind down, or trying to motivate ourselves to leave our nice warm bed. Being in bed accounts for one third of your day. That's fine, we need sleep. Being asleep for 8 hours is ideal. That leaves 16 hours to yourself in the day which is great. Except it isn't.

If you're in a 9-5 job, then that's another 8 hours gone. That's not taking into consideration people who do 12-hour shifts or people who run their own businesses.

Between sleep and work, that's 16 hours gone out of your 24hr day. That doesn't seem too bad. However, most people spent about an hour commuting to and from work. That's another 2 hours gone. Now we're down to 6.

Most people spend about an hour getting breakfast ready, an hour getting dinner ready, time cleaning up afterwards and a few small household chores. Now we're down to 4 hours.

If you're a parent, 2 hours will most likely be spent with your kids. If you're lucky, you might be able to get an hour's exercise in.

That brings us down to 2 hours of our own personal time in the day. That's if you're lucky.

Most of us spend that time either on our phones or watching TV. By the time we've spent the day running about at work and racing to and from work, we're so exhausted, we just need a break on the sofa.

For me, this is crazy. I do not want to waste my life dividing my time between a job and sleeping, especially a job I might not like.

I knew it wasn't an option to go off-grid and live off the land in the wilderness. Even then, I would have no money to travel, enjoy myself or go for outings with loved ones.

It was then I realised I needed a job to fund investments (and/or assets) that would, in turn, fund my retirement. During my research, I came across **F.I.R.E.** and instantly, I knew it was for me. It was everything I was looking for. The process of escaping the 9-5, creating multiple streams of income and reducing the dependency on a job, makes total sense to me. If we think about it, we have backup plans for everything in life, except a job. We have health insurance in case we become ill. We have mortgage repayment insurance in case we can't meet our payments for a certain length of time. However, very few people have a backup for their job.

A job is most people's single stream of income.

Most people only have savings to fall back on and even then, some people don't have that. F.I.R.E. teaches about financial independence and gaining freedom over your time. That was the biggest attraction to me:

The freedom to choose how to spend my whole day, not just 2 hours at the end of the day.

A brief history of F.I.R.E

The F.I.R.E idea originated in the early '90s. However, it took more than twenty years for the idea to spread and be known globally. Even now, it's not a common concept amongst many people. The roots of the F.I.R.E. movement can be traced back to Joe Dominguez and Vicki Robin, who published the book "Your Money or Your Life" in 1992. In its pages, Robin and Dominguez advocate for spending your retirement years enjoying time with friends, family and on hobbies instead of having to work well into your 60's. This became more of an issue because companies stopped providing stable pensions for employees, claiming it was a major drain on their funds.

At the core of F.I.R.E. is aggressive saving and investing. Many people hope to achieve F.I.R.E. by saving around 50% of their income. However, there are some extreme examples who save up to 75%. Their level of savings depends on their retirement goals.

Very simply, (as based on the Trinity study), the goal is to save enough money, then withdraw and live on 4% of the funds each year. When you reach that number, you have achieved financial independence and can retire early. Not everyone takes such extreme approaches to F.I.R.E. Some adherents like the general idea but they don't want to sacrifice some of life's daily pleasures. Due to this, different levels of F.I.R.E. were created to account for the different degrees of retirement levels. It also explains the different levels of sacrifices needed to achieve retirement goals. Below are the varying levels of retirement:

Fat F.I.R.E.

Fat F.I.R.E. focuses on building a large nest egg for retirement. The adherents wish to live an upper-middle-class lifestyle. Fat F.I.R.E. is a large number of investments. It is intended to maintain the same lifestyle that the person had before retirement. At this level, you maintain your standard of living.

Lean F.I.R.E.

Lean F.I.R.E. is for those who want to tackle financial independence from a frugal lens, choosing minimalist or anti-consumer lifestyles to achieve their goal. It is retiring, but reducing your standard of living during your retirement, from the current standard you have while working.

Barista F.I.R.E.

This approach to the F.I.R.E. movement is for those who plan to maintain a part-time job in retirement. Usually, the person receives enough money from their investments to cover their expenses. However, they still choose to work part-time in order to have spending money for leisure activities.

Coast F.I.R.E.

Coast F.I.R.E. is when your passive income is enough to pay for your expenditure but you would have nothing left over. Some people may reduce to a single working parent household at this stage. It is similar to a Barista F.I.R.E.

The biggest predictor of financial independence is the ability to delay gratification.

It's the ability to think about your future needs, and in doing so, resisting purchasing luxury items today. For example: the daily cup of coffee from your local coffee shop. Over time, through consistency and compound interest, you will have purchased your freedom.

F.I.R.E. is not about living a monk-like lifestyle. It's about living a minimalist lifestyle.

It's observing what you *actually* enjoy spending your money on and being true to yourself, rather than spending money on things you don't really enjoy.

For me, I like to travel. I wouldn't postpone travelling to a country because of the cost of flights. Instead, I would try to do it cheaply; picking the cheapest time of year to travel and the cheapest airline. I wouldn't spend the money on an expensive hotel as I have a low comfort level and would happily stay somewhere cheaper.

I would still go on the trip because I value the sense of adventure that comes with travelling to distant places. I always budget for holidays because they mean so much to me. Knowing how I feel about holidays, I don't have a problem resisting takeaway coffees or going for meals. I don't buy new clothes regularly because I don't really enjoy shopping!

Purchasing small daily pleasures doesn't mean much to me. I'd rather be able to travel the way I want and pick the destination I want.

For me, it's a constant decision to delay the minor pleasures now for the major pleasures later.

To quote the wise words of Richard G. Scott:

> *"Don't give up what you want most for what you want now."*

Be intentional with your time and effort. After a while, it becomes easier to be intentional. Once it becomes a habit, it's not even a conscious decision. It becomes effortless.

> *"(Financial) success is actually a short race—a sprint fueled by discipline just long enough for habit to kick in and take over."*
>
> *– Gary Keller*

Despite delaying minor pleasures, if there is a daily pleasure that brings you genuine enjoyment, I wouldn't sacrifice it. For example, my partner loves to have coffee on a daily basis. To deprive herself of that simple pleasure would hinder her life much more than the money she'd save. On the other hand, for me, sacrificing a daily coffee wouldn't be a big problem. My girlfriend has her coffee with friends, but she does cut back on her alcohol intake. She only really likes to drink when she's at a special occasion.

F.I.R.E. is about being self-aware. It's about appreciating the daily pleasures that bring you enjoyment. It's about being intentional with your money so that someday, you can buy your freedom.

I understand that financial independence isn't for everyone. Some people have no problem working for forty years in a job they enjoy. They would regard the idea of having so much free time as overwhelming. Some view their money as a reward. They feel they should spend it on anything they like, no matter how frivolous, in order to get them through the day. That's okay too. It's your life. If that's what makes you happy, then that's good.

However, I still think that financial awareness is a topic that should be on everyone's bucket list. Simply knowing how and what you spend your money on is a must. You can't achieve a bucket list without being financially aware and stable. You won't have the time to leave work or the resources to explore your interests without financial stability. For that reason, I've added it to my bucket list and I recommend that you do, too.

CHAPTER ELEVEN

To have love in your life

I PERSONALLY FEEL THAT everyone's bucket list should include striving to have love in their life.

Love has been defined by the Oxford dictionary as the "emotional and physiological bond we feel toward others, characterised by varying degrees of attraction, affection, intimacy, commitment and belongingness."

'Belongingness' refers to our desire to feel accepted by others and to have a sense of belonging to a group. Love is the attraction, intimacy, commitment and belonging we feel towards another individual and they feel towards us. To be the best person you can be, you need love in your life. Most of us only recognise love in the romantic sense; i.e. a wife, husband or partner. However, love can be experienced in many different relationships such as: familial love, friendship love and love of one's social group.

According to Maslow's hierarchy of needs, the need for love and belonging is number three on the pyramid. That's closely after the physiological need for food (number one) and the physiological need for safety (number two).

In my opinion, the need for love is just that; a 'need', rather than just a 'want'.

The first two are survival needs; the physiological need for food, water and shelter and the need for safety. If we don't have regular food, shelter, water and a place where we feel safe, it's very hard to have any zest for life.

The need for love and belonging is the first need that goes beyond survival mode. It sets you on the path to thrive, rather than just survive.

The goal of having a bucket list can help someone self-actualise, be the best they can be and be open to sharing and receiving love. Before setting a goal of having love in life, let's put love into a general term we can all understand.

Love can mean lots of things to lots of people. Love can be directed towards people or towards groups. Love can have varying levels and degrees.

Robert Sternberg describes love very accurately in his: "Triangular Theory of Love". Love can be understood by breaking it down into three core components which form a triangle. The triangle is used metaphorically and not literally.

The three components are:

- Intimacy
- Passion
- Commitment

Each component conveys a different aspect of love.

Intimacy: Intimacy refers to the feeling of belonging, closeness and connectedness in loving relationships. It's the emotional closeness one individual feels to another. It can be conveyed as the warmth you may have for someone. Intimacy often stems from long-standing relationships such as parents, long-time friends and long-time partners.

Passion: Passion refers to the romance, physical attraction and sexual desire in loving relationships. Passion consists mainly of physiological stimulus towards a person. That stimulus could be physical attraction, emotional attraction or primal sexual desire.

Commitment: Commitment has two components. The first is the choice that someone has made to love another. The second component is the commitment to maintain that love indefinitely. These two aspects of the commitment component do not necessarily come together. For example, someone can decide to love someone without being committed to loving them forever. Someone can also be committed to loving someone without acknowledging that they need to be in a relationship or need to be loved back by that person.

As summarised by Raj Raghunathan: "All of us have an intense desire to be loved and nurtured."

As children, our survival depended on us being loved and cared for by our parents. If our parents didn't love us, then they may abandon us and we would have to fend for ourselves. This was particularly life threatening before civilised societies were developed.

For this reason, the need to be loved is one of our most basic and fundamental needs as depicted in Maslow's hierarchy of needs. Due to the primary importance of the need to be loved, it's not surprising that many of us believe our happiness is largely based on feeling loved and cared for. If you are an adult, many believe that love should be from a partner and if a child, that love should be from your parents.

Some people believe that if they struggle to find a romantic partner by a certain age, it affects their self-worth. They may believe they're lacking success in romance, whereas another aspect of their life could be very successful, such as a career or education.

Love contributes to a feeling of happiness and contributes to self-worth. A lot of people are unaware that we need love to thrive as a human being, to self-actualise and to be the best we can be. One cannot be their best self without love in their life.

However, in our pursuit to be loved, many of us fail to acknowledge we have an equally important need: the need to love and care for others.

The need to love and care for others is just as strong as the need to be loved and nurtured. This is especially true if you feel you weren't adequately loved as a child. As a result, you may try to love your children more than you were, making sure they aren't deprived of the love you never got.

In a primal sense, you needed to be loved by your parents (and tribe) in order to survive. However, you also needed to love your parents when they got old. You also had to love and care for members of your tribe in order to help them survive. This occurred in an almost symbiotic relationship.

We know that the desire to love and care for others is hard-wired. Studies have shown that loving and caring for others increases our happiness levels. Projecting love and compassion for other people helps the recipient feel affection, but it also helps the person who sends it.

You might be asking: "If the need to love and care for others is hardwired and is such a powerful predictor of happiness, why don't we do it?" When we think about what makes us happy, most of us don't say "serving others" or "showering someone with love." Instead, we're likely to reply that "money" or "being loved" makes us happy.

In this modern era, we don't realise that we have a primal need to love and care for others because survival is no longer at stake. People do not need the tribe to love them, in order to survive. There are services such as retirement homes, food banks, charities and Social Services that fill the need the tribe once provided. People do not need a member of the tribe to hunt down the large game anymore. Instead, they can swing by the supermarket and pick up a leg of lamb in the refrigerated aisle. When they are sick, they don't need a member of the tribe to love and care for them. Instead, they can pick up the phone to their doctor, a complete stranger who will care for them. For the above reasons, we don't need to emotionally commit to people in order to receive care and support. As a result, apart from our family and close relationships, we are much more distant from the wider community.

With regard to our lack of desire to reach out and help others, another contributor could be due to societal messages. Society and consumerism tell us that our happiness lies in being the recipient of a partner's attention and love. This is based on the premise of having to buy consumer products to fulfil these desires. The rise in consumerism and advertising has targeted our basic human needs and changed them. This causes a mass culture change in how we think we will get our basic needs met.

A few generations ago, our parents and grand-parents didn't have much; just their house, a small farm (or menial job) and a handful of kids. Now, there are more products and luxuries available. This has created a sense of selfishness among the recent generation as they think they need these products to be happy and to feel loved. People now focus on what they need and desire, rather than on what they can give to others. A lot of millennials and younger genera-tions believe that happiness lies in achieving self-enhancing goals such as career success, wealth, fame, or power. In contrast, the need to love and care for others is rarely emphasised.

So, we have realised that love is a basic human need. We need to feel loved and cared for as it increases our self-worth and also our happiness. With increased self-esteem and happiness, we can thrive and get as close as we can to self-actualisation. We are now aware that we also have an equally important need to love and care for others, which also increases our happiness and ability to self-actualise.

With that in mind, how does that relate to creating a bucket list which will help us to be the best we can be?

It is apparent that we need love in our life; both giving and receiving. We can't control who gives us love, whether that's a parent or a partner. Some people, hardened by traumatic events in life, aren't capable of giving us love when we need it. However, we can control the amount of love we give to others. We can adjust our behaviour to love and care for others. We can influence others to love us by being a generous and kind person. The two behaviours are closely linked. By being kind, you are most likely generous. If you are generous, you are also kind. This will work in a very cyclical way. By being generous, you will be a happier, kinder person. In turn, this will help you to show more affection towards others through your generous acts. The receiver of your generosity will feel more loved and will likely return the feelings of love. You will then have satisfied your need to love and your need to be loved. All through a very small behaviour of generosity.

On a separate note, let's not confuse the act of generosity with financial generosity. You can be generous without giving money. You can give something more important than money, such as your time. You can babysit your sister's kids so she can go out with her husband. You can be a listening ear when someone needs to off-load their worries. Listening is one of the most sought-after forms of generosity. Yes, of course you can lend money to someone. However, let's not mistake financial generosity as a means of appeasing one's conscience.

> *"To give money to a sufferer is only a come-off. It is only a postponement of the real payment, a bribe paid for silence, a credit system in which a paper promise to pay answers for the time instead of liquidation. We owe to man higher succours than food and fire. We owe to man."*
>
> *– Ralph Waldo Emerson*

Sometimes we practise financial generosity, whether that's a monthly direct debit to a charity or dropping some change in a homeless guy's pot. Rather than wanting to better that person's life, the intention might be to make us feel better about ourselves. It might quieten our conscience for a moment while we witness the suffering going on around us. As Emerson points out, giving a few euros to a homeless guy could pay for the silence of our minds.

When we donate to charities, we don't question how that money will be spent. Nor do we question a homeless man as to how our contribution will be spent—whether that's on food, drugs or alcohol. Personally, I don't give money to homeless people on the street. When they ask for money however, I offer to get them something to eat. I have gotten an array of responses. The ones who are truly in need take the food. The ones who don't want food, just want me to enable their destructive habits.

However, by making more of an effort, talking to them and listening, I am truly trying to help. I'm not just giving them loose change; I'm giving my time. Time to listen, ask what food they want and buy it for them. I am building their belief in kindness, not their belief in money.

When you donate money, don't let it provide a justification not to have to give your time or your listening ear.

How does generosity result in you becoming happier?

There are three main reasons why people who carry out acts of true, time-spent generosity, experience higher levels of happiness.

Firstly, people have a natural predisposition to act fairly towards other people. People who receive an act of generosity feel a moral obligation to reciprocate it. When someone does something nice for you, you want to do something nice for them in return. This is called the **Law of Reciprocity.** When you are generous to others, you attract generous behaviour from them in return. By being generous, you will give the feeling of love but you will also be more likely to receive a feeling of love.

Secondly, there is a phenomenon known as homophily. **Homophily** is the tendency for people to seek out, or be attracted to, those who are similar to themselves. When you are generous, you increase the chances of attracting others who are generous. Creating a social circle with like-minded, generous and compassionate people will bring you more happiness. Spending more time with generous, kind people, rather than socialising with selfish individuals, will increase your level of happiness.

Finally, (and possibly most importantly), being generous enhances your ability to give and receive love because of how you think of yourself. When you perform a generous act, you feel happier within yourself. Your self-esteem increases due to the fact you are bringing joy into the world. You feel proud of yourself and hold yourself in higher regard. You know deep-down:

"I am a good person, or at least, I am trying to be."

From these internal conversations, you develop more self-worth and realise you are worthy of love. You are someone that deserves to be loved, whether you have received it yet or not. From this self-awareness, you are more likely to continue being generous. You can give love to others without the fear of rejection. As such, you will receive much more love than you have in the past.

On your bucket list, it's a good idea to set one of your goals as:

"To be generous to others until you believe you are worthy of love."

If you already have this belief, that's great. However, think carefully about whether you actually believe this, deep down.

If you do believe it, then your goal could be: "to be a consistently generous person".

Whilst being generous, remember it is more important to do small things with great love, than to do great things with little love as stated by Mother Teresa.

"Not all of us can do great things, but we can do small things with great love."

– Mother Teresa

You don't have to go volunteering for a week every year, you just need to be generous when opportunities present themselves. These opportunities will present themselves on a daily basis. As a result, you will have daily opportunities to give and receive love, become a better person and feel worthy of love.

Delaying gratification

Endeavouring to write a bucket list which will help you to become the best person you can be is no mean feat. It will take persistence and consistency for years. In fact, it's a lifestyle choice, not just a goal. Due to the extensive commitment required, the individual who takes this path must have an immense desire to change, grow and develop. It is this desire that will buffer against any setback and will help to build a sense of resilience.

Napoleon Hill conveyed this desire as an important factor in attaining goals in his book: "Think and grow rich". Napoleon Hill was a journalist who studied the top 500 millionaires at that time, including Henry Ford, Charles M. Schwab and Andrew Carnegie. His book was the result of several years of research and interviews. His best-seller was produced in 1937 and is still a top-selling financial book to this day. Napoleon stated that one of the most prominent contributors to success and wealth was **desire.**

Hill stated that the key to success was to: "define a very clear and measurable goal".

Then: "invest all your willpower into achieving it".

It may take many years before you succeed, however, if you hold on to your desire, you will eventually attain it. This sounds like common sense:

> *"Know what you want and then go for it."*

However, how often do we set a goal, then commit to it, to the point of no return?

How often do we set a goal and continue with it, despite being subjected to criticism, disbelief and ridicule?

How often do we give up on our goals for the sake of conformity or lack of inner belief?

I've lost count of the amount of times I've been criticised for following my goals: meditating daily, not eating meat, travelling to countries off the beaten path, putting myself into challenging situations, facing fear, skydiving, boxing, starting an Airbnb business and trying to self-develop at a young age.

Your bucket list will be no different. Your bucket list goals will be the process by which you will become a better person. If you attempt to develop in a society that doesn't promote personal development, but promotes consumerism, you'll be going against the grain. You will be criticised at times, but that's okay. You cannot be exceptional by doing the same things as average people. However, you must have an overwhelming desire to achieve your bucket list and be your best self. The mind is built to conform to those around you. You mustn't bend to its will.

Remember your intentions with your goals and remember why you are on this path.

It was easy for me to remember my goals. My personal belief is that I have one shot to live the best life. I'm not going to waste it. I don't believe in an afterlife, nor do I think there is a heaven or hell. I base life on what is around me in the world, for example, nature. Things live, grow and die. Their nutrients return to the earth and from that, organisms grow again. However, the same organism doesn't return. The nutrients replenished new life.

This doesn't have to be your belief; however you should have a clear vision of what you want to achieve in your lifetime. There will be obstacles in your way, but no matter how long it takes, or how many setbacks, with a clear vision, you will achieve your goals. Start with the end in mind.

What kind of person do you want to be in old age? What do you want to have achieved by the end of your life? What will the people you love say about you when you pass?

_____

_____

_____

Think about it, obsess about it. Set goals that will lead to this outcome. Attack these goals with an unworldly desire. It is this desire that Hill promoted for the attainment of goals; relentless and unwavering.

However, you *will* waver... we all do, but we don't stop, even in times of contemplation. Stick to the process until you regain your strength. The first way to cultivate this level of desire is through your thoughts.

Thoughts are real and produce action. Think about what you want to achieve in your life and the person you want to be. Think about it in minute detail. Obsess about it and let your thoughts run free. Do this until your goal is clear and all your questions are answered. This can then be cemented through the use of affirmations. Affirmations create a desire in your subconscious, thanks to the process of auto-suggestion. Desire will lead to success.

"Whatever the mind can conceive and believe, it can achieve."

– Napoleon Hill

A structured way of accomplishing this is by following a 6-step process:

1. Define the **characteristics** of the person you want to be and what you want to have achieved.

_____

_____

2. Determine what you are willing to **sacrifice** to achieve this goal (eg. money, time, nights out etc.)

_____

3. Choose a **measurable date** to recognise progress. Set goal dates for tasks you want to have completed and dates for sights you want to have visited

_____

4. Choose the **order** in which you want to tackle them (note: this may change as time goes on). For the first one, create a plan of how to achieve your goal. Begin at once, whether you feel ready or not. Read this book, write your bucket list and attack your goals.

---

5. Write all of the above down in a **clear statement.** Read this written statement aloud, twice a day; first thing in the morning and last thing at night. Do this for several weeks until it is embedded in your mind.

---

6. Then **fall in love** with the process. You will love and respect yourself more with each task you complete. Love yourself even when you're starting out, but you will love yourself more as you achieve each goal. Don't wait to be happy or fulfilled. Be happy and love yourself more each day because the list may never be completed. It is the process that is causing change, not ticking words off a piece of paper.

Giving up maladaptive coping strategies

The process of obtaining self-actualisation involves adding or enhancing our personal traits.

That could involve getting a new perspective, adding intentionality or acquiring a plan to become financially independent. We try to add qualities to ourselves as a means of self-improvement, which will get us closer to self-actualisation. However, an equal amount of progress can be made by quitting a bad habit, just as much as acquiring a good quality.

All of us have bad habits: swearing, smoking, gambling, or being late are just some examples. The most potent and harmful habits are formed as coping strategies or a means to satisfy basic human needs. Previously, we discussed Maslow's hierarchy of needs:

225

The first four levels of the pyramid are the deficiency needs.

Deficiency needs can cause physical and psychological discomfort if they are not met. The motivation to fulfil these needs gets stronger, the longer they are unfulfilled. Coping strategies, formed to meet these needs, are the most detrimental to us.

For example, we all have the physiological need for intimacy, as well as the emotional need for belongingness and love (as seen on level 3 of the pyramid).

I have worked with people who have formed a maladaptive coping strategy for intimacy and belonging. Usually, their parents were never really affectionate. There were usually very little hugs, kisses or soothing from their parents. In addition to this I found the parents of these young people to lack emotional support and be more prone to giving practical support. What happened to these young people, but particularly young men, when they started college or finished secondary school? They would have a great desire (as well as a fear) of intimacy. A lot of these young men set out with their desire for intimacy combined with a hyper sexualised society and they engaged in womanising or being hyper sexual.

At this point, some of you might be thinking: "Is this not the same for every young man or woman in their late teens and early twenties?"

In some sense, you are right. However, it is a problem when it affects the quality of their life. For these young people, it didn't matter how good a night they had, how fun or crazy it was, if they didn't 'pull', it was a failure. If they didn't hook up in several weeks, their self-worth was on the floor. They also couldn't take rejection because that would confirm their innermost fears that they didn't deserve intimacy. To avoid the fear of rejection, they drink heavily or do drugs. That way, if they are rejected, they won't remember or feel it. That often leads to a dependency on alcohol or substances.

Most came to recognise their problem when other young people were in secure relationships, while they were still looking for one-night stands. Some became aware and saw that this was a **maladaptive coping strategy** and looked at the causes.

Amongst the young people I worked with, it often stemmed back to unmet needs in childhood. Once we identified their unmet needs, some were able to have a conversation with their parents about it. In some cases, this took weeks, months or even years before the opportunity presented itself in natural conversation. In most cases, their parents were unaware of their lack of affection or emotional support. In their opinion, they had actually given more affection than they had received from their parents. The conversation did not always fix anything directly but it allowed the young person to start to understand that the lack of affection was not their fault. They began to see they *are* worthy of love and that they *are* loved.

Then they needed to implement practical changes to stop the maladaptive behaviour. They often restructured friendship groups and stepped away from "party friends"; mates who only wanted to go out drinking. They tried to befriend people who truly cared for them. That usually only came to fruition when they themselves started to be a better friend and show that they care for other people without the fear of rejection. Showing they really cared for their friends and expressing it, put them in a vulnerable position. However, it was only from that starting point that they could find out who was there for them.

Following this, they started giving relationships a chance and allowed an emotional connection to form. That took a while and there were probably a few broken hearts along the way. Some met their life partners and others are still searching. However, they are no longer using those maladaptive coping strategies and placing barriers in their own way.

Some of you may think that this is just a part of growing up and it is. However, how many people *don't* emotionally grow up? How many people continue to have maladaptive coping strategies for one basic human need or another? Whether that's drugs and alcohol to hide a lack of self-worth or hanging around with the wrong crowd just to have a sense of belonging. We all have one or two maladaptive coping strategies. As part of your bucket list, you should identify, address, alter or remove your most maladaptive coping strategy. Relinquish the hold it has on you and your life.

Look at Maslow's hierarchy of needs to see if there are any stages where you have been lacking in the past. Address it and set a plan for how you can change it.

Maybe your mother had some bad boyfriends. Maybe they would shout, roar and trash the house. Perhaps you didn't feel safe and secure in childhood (as shown in level 2). You should have that conversation with your mother. It doesn't have to be a blame game, but for you to move on, your inner child needs to feel heard. You can listen to your mother's side. You can accept her apology or not, the choice is yours. After that, you need to see how you will address the situation differently when you are a mother.

Perhaps you will decide not to have kids until you are in a secure relationship. If you get a new partner, you might decide to date for six months before you introduce them to your children. Once the plan is set, history won't repeat itself.

It's important to look at how the situation affected you internally. Are you a nervous person now? Do you not trust men? Do you have a habit of dating similar men?

Identify the habit and alter it to a more beneficial behaviour. Remove the past behaviours from your life. This is a lot easier said than done. It can take years to overcome, but it will be one of the most worthwhile accomplishments on your bucket list.

Also, just for the record, I had more than one maladaptive coping strategy and so may you. If, like me, you have more than one, then it can seem overwhelming. If you have several bad habits, use the snowball effect. Start with the smallest and easiest habit. After you remove it, you will have a sense of reward and achievement. You can use that positive energy to tackle the next one, and so on.

This is perhaps the most difficult task on the list. It may take weeks, months or even years, but your list is not complete without them. You won't be whole unless you remove them.

Mistakes, setbacks and accountability

As we strive to be the best we can be, we will inevitably falter, stumble, or even blatantly fail in our endeavours. I have failed so many times in my personal life. In particular, I have failed so many times when trying to conquer my fear of water. I jumped in, panicked and freaked out. I tried scuba diving and panicked when my mask filled with water. I didn't really go into the water until I was in my mid-twenties. I also struggled with my personal development. I wasn't a naturally patient person. As someone who was incredibly motivated, I put in a lot of effort and expected others to have the same standards. If they couldn't meet those standards through effort or ability, I was intolerant. It took me years to tackle this. Even then, I only really tackled it when it caused me tension in the workplace as a manager. Staff mentioned that my tone was aggressive when speaking to staff and it was. I couldn't hide my frustration when there was a problem. My tone deepened and my voice became sharp and blunt. As far as I was concerned, I was just going into problem-solving mode. I simply wanted the information I needed from them as soon as possible in order to solve the problem. I would form a solution, then bluntly present them with the information they needed to solve their problem. However, I didn't consider how my tone came across. This attitude, combined with my disposition to enjoy a good debate, made me rather non-approachable. My approach appeared uncompassionate. I was applying a logical problem-solving approach whilst working with people who are, by nature, emotional beings. I was applying logic to an emotional situation.

As human beings, we are far more emotional than logical. If humans were one hundred percent logical, we would stop using fossil fuels, stop overfishing and try to prevent climate change. However, that action would result in a loss of jobs for many people. The emotion which would arise from that is fear. Rich people would lose a lot of money, which stems from their deep-rooted greed. People also try to avoid discomfort as much as possible, opting to prevent uncomfortable feelings and instead, remain within their comfort zone.

Who wants to give up their car and live in a cold house for several years (maybe even decades) until our sustainable energy crisis is solved?

These are some emotions that hinder every logical process. It is why governments spend most of their time steering away from a direct solution to problems. Instead, they try to find a solution that people will accept because it provides the least discomfort.

Most situations that deal with people are emotional situations. To refute this is to declare that people are robots.

The situation that I discussed above was during my first management role. To be honest, I was mirroring the values of the company, but I wasn't projecting my own personal values of fairness. I was a bad manager, but a good employee. I believed I was right and the staff were the problem. This type of thinking is generally behind a lot of disputes between people. It's the "us versus them" mentality. In that mind frame, it's difficult to accept any argument from the other person as they're not "in our group". We disregard everything they say. However, we don't learn anything when we have this mentality because we're not taking accountability for our actions. It is only when you take accountability that you can learn from every situation. You can use every experience for personal growth.

As Steve Shallenberger said: *"You steadily grow into becoming your best as you choose to be accountable and accept responsibility (for your actions)."*

This has transformed my life. I learned from those mistakes. I still learn daily from my mistakes instead of aimlessly wandering through life blaming others.

By taking accountability, you will slowly evolve from having an external locus of control to an internal locus of control. An external locus of control is someone who believes that external factors control their success. They say things like:

> *"With this economy, I just can't get a good job."*
> *"You have to have money to make money."*
> *"It's easy for them; they got help from their dad."*
> *"I won't get the promotion. The boss likes Bill more than me because he's funny and I'm not."*

According to these people, their success is out of their control. They're at the whim of the universe and society. They believe they have little or no power when it comes to achieving their goals.

Meanwhile, a person with an internal locus of control believes they have a high level of control over the outcome of their life. They believe that if they work hard and work smart, they will get what they want. They believe they have the capacity to learn new skills and deal with challenging situations. They are the master of their own destiny. They know that some factors are out of their control, but with time and perseverance, they will succeed eventually.

To be the best you can be, you must have an internal locus of control. View yourself as a master of your own fate. To do that, you must take accountability for your part in every situation, both good and bad. You might be thinking: "Well, sometimes bad things happen and it's just not my fault." That is one hundred percent true, sometimes bad things do happen. However, sometimes you might play a minimal role in that negative situation. There might be a situation that you have to learn from.

For example, my friends allowed one of their mates to move into their house, knowing that he occasionally takes drugs at the weekend. He promised that he wouldn't take drugs in their house and that it wouldn't affect their lifestyle. However, his drug problem turned out to be a lot bigger than my friends realised. In fact, he did end up taking drugs in their house. They kicked him out and their friendship broke down.

Following this incident, they spent quite a bit of time complaining about him. In their mind, he was to blame; he made a promise and he broke it. He was taking illegal drugs on a regular basis in their home when he had initially claimed he only used recreationally at weekends. He ruined their friendship.

In this scenario, they are mostly correct. However, if they took accountability for their part in a bad situation, they would have to admit that they knowingly allowed a drug user to stay in their home, thereby putting their friendship in jeopardy. Going forward, they should learn from that situation.

You must take accountability and learn from every situation that comes your way in order to maximise your personal development. The hardest time to take accountability is when misery comes your way through tragedy.

For example, how do you take accountability if your child is killed in a car accident where the vehicle skid on black ice? Your child was twenty-one years old. They knew how to drive and they needed to drive to work even though the roads were icy. That's no one's fault and it wouldn't do you any favours to take accountability. In these circumstances, all you are accountable for is how you react to this tragedy. Yes, you will be stricken with grief, but a day will come when you have to be accountable for how you are going to continue to live your life. Are you going to be miserable forever? Are you going to turn to drink and become an alcoholic? Are you going to deny yourself happiness because your child is no longer alive? Even in tragedy, after we deal with the emotions, we must be accountable for our actions and how we are going to continue our life. This is one of the hardest tests of life in my opinion, but some people have done wonderful things with their accountability to better this world.

Accountability is a key component of self-actualisation and success. When we take accountability for our actions (or the part we played), it allows us to derive learning from every situation. This makes every negative situation a catalyst for change in the future. When this becomes our day-to-day practice, we draw closer to being the best person we can be. Alternatively, when we don't take accountability, but instead blame others for our faults, it disempowers us.

Mahatma Gandhi said: "It is wrong and immoral to seek to escape the consequences of one's acts."

That is what we are doing when we are blaming others—escaping the consequences of our own actions. We aren't owning up to the consequences for our part played in a situation. There are situations when others will be more at fault than you are, however that shouldn't prevent you from taking accountability for your own actions in that situation. Children often do this. They blame others, (usually their siblings or school friends), taking no accountability for what they did. That's all well and good in childhood, but if this continues into adulthood, then you have an individual who constantly blames others and never takes accountability for anything.

People who don't take accountability for their actions are often unaware of the power of their actions. As such, they have an external locus of control. When they notice other people's success, they believe those people must have something they haven't got. When they see someone else with their own business, a good job or well-mannered kids, they scoff inwardly. They say things like: "It's alright for them. I never got the opportunity to go to business school. I didn't come from money."

That person has an external locus of control and will constantly struggle to take charge of their life. They have a victim mindset. Life happens to them rather than them happening to life.

Be wise as you manoeuvre through life.

> *"Wisdom stems from personal accountability. We all make mistakes; own them… learn from them. Don't throw away the lesson by blaming others."*
>
> *– Steve Maraboli*

Once you start to take accountability, you learn from every situation, especially negative ones. Once you learn, you become wise and avoid such situations in the future. Once you are wise, you can be free:

- *Free from making mistakes over and over again.*
- *Free from blame.*

- *Free from deflection.*
- *Free from lying to yourself.*

This freedom allows you to become self-aware. Once we take accountability, we learn about ourselves; our weaknesses and our strengths. Once we are self-aware, we can choose a path in life which will help us to be happy and free.

When I took accountability for my actions, I realised I was mirroring a company's values that I didn't support. I left and found another company whose values were more in line with my own. This forced me to move from one sector to another, which actually became one of the best decisions I ever made. It was only through taking accountability that I became self-aware and had the ability to make the necessary changes. Once in that role, I thrived. I was the youngest manager in the company and had some of the best outcomes regarding my cases with young people. I even surprised myself and finally felt I was meeting my potential.

> *"It is only when you take (accountability) for your life that you discover how powerful you truly are".*
>
> *– Alannah Hunt*

Take accountability every day and realise how powerful you really are!

Be ready to learn from your travels

When travelling, we shouldn't focus solely on the sights themselves. Rather, we should focus on the experiences we have from setting off on an adventure; leaving our familiar routine, lifestyle, house and country.

These bouts of travelling or sightseeing lead to learning of the self. We rarely give ourselves time to reflect on our lives. We're too busy working, shopping, eating out or watching TV to have the time for self-reflection. To rectify this, we should adhere to the wise words of Mahatma Gandhi:

> *"Live as if you were to die tomorrow. Learn as if you were to live forever."*

In order to make this quote relatable, I would translate it as follows: To live like you would die tomorrow doesn't mean that you should go out on a drinking session, throw morality to one side and be a slave to your basic desires (of sex, pleasure or violence). It means getting perspective: observing what is important in your life and trying to structure your life around it. This mirrors the above chapter 'Values', where we should try to live in conjunction with our values.

If family is something you value strongly, try making it a regular occurrence to meet up with family members. If you like dancing, then make sure you find a dance class and attend regularly, regardless if you're going with a friend or by yourself. I have often gone to a dance class or a martial art class by myself. It actually makes you more approachable to other people. They are more willing to talk to someone who is standing alone than trying to muscle in on a small group of people.

Live as though it's your last day on earth, cherish each day as though it's your last and structure your life around what you love.

The second half of the quote: "Learn as if you were to live forever" recognises that we will never reach a stage of knowing everything. We will continue to learn until the day we die.

Do not let the achievable stop you from learning the most important subject of all:

The subject of thy self.

You must know yourself and love yourself.

To truly know yourself, you must test yourself. Like any scientific experiment, to truly understand any element, you must subject it to adverse conditions.

That is what travelling will do to you.

At times it will be good, at times it will be great. You will have some of the best times of your life, but you will also struggle.

You may jump on a night bus from Toronto to Quebec, end up on an aisle seat and realise that you've forgotten your neck pillow. You might end up walking around with a crick in your neck for two weeks.

You might try to travel by bus from Minsk to Ukraine, but get stopped at the border by armed guards. They won't let you pass through, even though you're a European citizen returning to a European country. Your visa was granted because you flew into the country but now you have to fly out. No-one at the Consulate told you any different, despite speaking to them twice.

You might be suffering from food poisoning whilst trying to walk up those never-ending steps in Dubrovnik, with the thoughts: "God, kill me now" hammering around your head.

You might be abused in various languages by locals in various countries for reasons you still don't know to this day.

These scenarios have all happened to me and they have taught me so much.

Firstly, they have taught me to be prepared for life.

Fail to prepare: prepare to have your neck in agony. Work out your own due diligence when you're about to embark on a journey. It's your responsibility to prepare yourself—you can't rely on the instruction of others.

If something happens and it's out of your control, accept it.

When we were stopped at the border of Ukraine, we had to get back on a bus and return to Minsk before getting a flight to Ukraine. We slept most of the way and lost almost a day of our trip, but we never got mad or stressed. We just had to accept it. It's now become a funny story to tell.

In Dubrovnik, I learned to be suspicious of meat-based meals that arrive at your table too soon. Sometimes it's not always the big things that knock you in life! Sometimes it's as simple as some uncooked chicken, a flight of stairs and a hard-to-undo belt buckle.

No matter what your age, no matter where you travel; you will learn something about yourself on your trip. As long as you have a sight to see, a goal to achieve and time to reflect, you will develop each time you travel. By getting a plane, train, bus or car, you will develop. Travelling frees up your mind to think about yourself and your life. You finally have the time to ask yourself questions about your life. It gives you the opportunity to reflect and change the direction of your life, if need be.

On each trip, whether you're a carefree teen or an elder in the final chapter of life, you learn something different. In every stage of life, there are still days to be lived and obstacles to be faced.

We have a direction that we want to go in life and values we must try to align with.

Finally, we want to deal with obstacles in life with dignity and self-respect.

- None of this comes without self-reflection.
- Self-reflection only comes with time.
- Time is something we give away in this fast-paced life.

Nowadays, people struggle to give time to self-reflection. That is, until they see the importance of it.

The most realistic way for people to self-reflect in modern times is to travel. It's not the easiest, cheapest or even the best way to self-reflect, but it is the most socially acceptable way to push yourself out of your comfort zone and give yourself adequate time to reflect on your life.

Learning through travel

As previously stated, every time you travel, you're leaving your comfort zone; the familiarity of your own country and your network of friends. In doing so, there will be times when you're placed in stressful situations. However, these are exactly the kind of experiences that will help you to become the person you strive to be.

- Travelling can bring you closer to self-actualisation.
- Travelling will give you time to self-reflect.
- Travelling will throw obstacles your way that you will learn to overcome.

When travelling, you don't have that comfort blanket; the network of support that you have at home. This forces you to trust yourself and depend on your own resources. Over time, this will eventually lead to a deeper sense of loving and accepting yourself (if you haven't already reached this point).

Below are a few snippets of lessons I've learnt during various trips. I hope they highlight the range of personal development that can be achieved from travelling.

Denmark

My first ever trip was to Copenhagen, Denmark when I was nineteen years old. I was visiting a friend via the Erasmus programme. At that time, I was due to travel to Canada six weeks later. I would be in Canada for six months as part of the exchange programme through my university degree.

Most of my friends were planning to go to universities in Europe, which would only require a short plane flight if they needed to return home.

I hasten to add that my decision to choose Canada was not out of some huge sense of bravado or immense courage. Rather, I simply hadn't submitted my request on time, so there were no other spaces available nearby.

I suddenly realised that I'd never gone anywhere by myself, so perhaps a practice trip would be a good idea. After all, I was about to cross the Atlantic with absolutely no support structure in place.

I arranged to stay with a friend in Copenhagen for five days and took my first flight, all by myself.

Arriving in Copenhagen, my friend was unable to collect me from the airport, but advised that I should get the subway to Lindevang, where she was staying.

Being young and dependent on others, I hadn't bought any credit for my phone. This was the time before you could use your mobile data anywhere in Europe. Setting off, I naively presumed all subways were underground. Too nervous to ask anyone if I was on the right train, I jumped on (what I thought) was a very train-like subway.

Finally, I summoned up the courage to ask someone if I was on the right train. They told me that I was on a train to Sweden. The next stop would be the last one within Denmark before it went on to Malmo, Sweden.

Horrified, I jumped off and made my way back to the airport. This time, I got on the subway which was the tram line running both over and under-ground. I reached the desired stop, nearly an hour later than I had planned, just as my friend was about to give up waiting for me.

She told me that if I hadn't turned up when I did, she would have given up and went home. That would have been catastrophic for me. With no phone credit, I wouldn't have been able to contact her. Roaming data didn't work in other countries at that time. She hadn't given me her postal address at that stage either, so I would have been screwed. I guess I would probably have had to go back to the airport in order to use their free WIFI.

From this, I learned how dependent I was on others. I expected my friend to collect me from the airport and take care of me. I was dependent on other people and didn't take accountability. As a result, that was something that started to change after that trip. I became much more prepared and independent; not just regarding trips but with other aspects of my life.

After that incident, I spent the next few days being shown around Copenhagen by my own private tour guide. It was then that I started to fall in love with sightseeing and got a sense of adventure from exploring a new city. That sense of adventure was only previously quenched from sport and drinking, never anything else. Prior to that trip, I imagined that travelling was a waste of time and money. After that trip, I relished the notion that I had another six months ahead to travel more.

After seeing beautiful castles, partying in a butcher shop in the meatpacking district, smoking for the first time in Christiania and drinking as much Carlsberg as possible while dressed as a sailor on Halloween, I was left in awe of travelling. However, I was disappointed by my naivety and my rigid view of the world. I may have

become an adult legally, but not by capability.
From this trip, I was enlightened. I felt steered
towards independence and all that it encum-
bered.

Canada

Several weeks later, I went to Canada. My anxiety
was sky-high and I hadn't slept properly in two
weeks. Would I cope being away from home for
so long? The longest I had been away from home
was three weeks when I stayed in an Irish college
for the summer. Even then, my parents were only
an hour and a half away by car and they visited
on weekends.

This time, I knew I didn't have the money to fly
back home if I was homesick. By getting on that
flight, I was going past the point of no return.

This time, I was more prepared. Family friends
collected me from the airport in Toronto. I stayed
in their house that first evening and they dropped
me off at my college apartment the following day.
They even helped me with my grocery shopping.
Considering I was practically a stranger to them,
they were incredibly generous and helpful
people.

During that time, I learned how to get out of my
comfort zone and make friends. After all, I had to.
During those six months, I learned so much about

becoming independent. The 'sink-or-swim' experience made me the independent man I am today.

There were many small, but significant experiences, which slowly increased my independence during those six months. I think I would be a completely different person, had I not taken that trip. Remember, I only went to Canada because I was too late to apply for anywhere in Europe.

I would like to highlight the most valued lesson during that trip. I started the semester in January and we met the other international students on our first day. There was another girl from Ireland called Kate who I became friendly with. We became acquainted with an outspoken Australian student who was a few years older than us. The Australian befriended a Swedish guy. The Swedish guy was much quieter and actually rather submissive to him. In a way, it was almost as though he had become his second-in-command or sidekick. We hung out with them for the first week, along with another Australian who was so laid back, he was practically horizontal.

During that first week, we went to the mall, to see if it lived up to the hype we had seen on TV.

The outgoing Australian shuffled us into a travel agent to book a group spring break in less than ten weeks' time. He was keen to go ahead and book the trip that day. His 'Yes-man' Swedish sidekick was of course egging him on, agreeing with everything he said.

I think we all got caught up in the excitement—we were young, we were in a new country and we were led by an older guy who had more brawn than brains.

Needless to say, we went ahead and booked a trip to Cancun together, even though we had only known each other for five days.

As the weeks rolled on and the spring break was fast approaching, our friendships had already drifted apart. The outgoing Australian and his Swedish sidekick had drifted off into their own intense duo. The Irish girl and I only spent limited time together which was mostly mediated by the laid-back Australian. The Irish girl desperately wanted to be friends with the Australian and the Swede, yet was constantly hurt by their rejection. It was a poor decision to plan a trip without really knowing each other. However, being young, dumb and too skint to cancel, we all went ahead with the trip.

Being Irish and feeling the need to live up to the stereotype, I got blackout drunk on Rum and Coke with the laid-back Australian, after generously tipping the Mexican bartender (as we had been advised to do). Sure enough, there could be thirty people waiting for a drink, but thanks to our tip, he would serve us the moment we hit the bar.

We were blackout drunk by 2pm in the afternoon.

The Australian and Swede, annoyed by our behaviour, bitched and moaned about us to the Irish girl, who, craving their approval, agreed.

The following morning, I woke at 5am, having passed out at some stage the night before. My hangover was horrific and the atmosphere was stiff.

I apologised profusely before we set off on our makeshift friendship for the week.

I wasn't comfortable drinking or getting too drunk in case the group excommunicated me. It was spring break in Cancun. I was in one of the most beautiful places in the world, during the prime of my life, feeling absolutely miserable.

I was with people who didn't care if I was there or not. They would leave the club and head home without checking to see if I was coming too. It's hard to have a good time when you're nineteen years old, and too afraid to get drunk in case you end up alone and vulnerable in a nightclub packed with strangers.

My confidence was rocked. I had made mistakes; I was with people I didn't trust in a country I wasn't familiar with. I felt more alone than ever.

Nonetheless, it's during the darkest times that we learn the most.

I learned that you have to take responsibility for your own actions, although it might have been a few years later before I truly grasped this concept.

By taking accountability, you can learn from every experience, thereby developing as a person.

I also learned that you can be in the best place in the world, but if you're with the wrong people, it can be hell.

I learned about the importance of the people I surround myself with.

Jim Rohn famously said: *"You're the average of the five people you spend the most time with."*

From then on, I've been much more selective about who I spend my time with and who is in my inner circle.

Interrailing through Europe

Two years later, I went interrailing across Europe with my two friends. At twenty-one years old, one of my friends was a bit younger than me and had just come out of a five-year relationship.

By then, I had become more independent and was much more prepared, having planned the entire trip before setting off.

To be honest, my friends were basically passengers on my trip—I had decided where we were going and what we were going to see. We went to Berlin, Prague, Vienne, Bratislava, Lake Bled, Budapest and Krakow. We then went back to Budapest to attend Europe's largest festival 'Ziget'.

I learned so much during that five-week trip;

- how much I love routine and exercise,
- how to conquer sleep and not rely on alcohol
- how to be patient when bad things happen (such as getting on the wrong bus).

I saw the most beautiful sights and had one of the best times of my life. Probably the best lesson of all was realising that there's more to life than working, studying and paying bills. I valued the time I had spent travelling and knew it would be rare to have that amount of free time again.

My eyes had been opened to the beauty in the world. From Charles Bridge in Prague, to the scenic lake and hills of Lake Bled, to the Ruin Bars of Budapest, it was beautiful. Seeing scenic places seemed to almost heal me. It made me feel happy and allowed me to put perspective on my life.

I was hooked on travelling and knew I wanted to have adventures like this for the rest of my life.

After reading about the "6 universal psychological needs" by Tony Robbins, I learned that I have a high need for uncertainty. I was aware I craved adventure more than the average person. I was also aware that, being a highly conscientious person, I needed to set goals for myself. I need to strive for achievements, not out of vanity, but because I feel I am my best self when I'm in the process of achieving a goal. I am more focused and more resilient. I find it easier to delay gratification and resist temptations when I have something to strive for. For the next few years, my goals were about sightseeing and travelling, but gradually, my goals changed to become more intrinsic and centred around values.

I have a few funny travel stories to tell; incidents that provided humour as well as great lessons.

My friend came on a trip with me. He had never shown any prior interest in travelling or any latent desire to leave his comfort zone. However, he pestered me to let him come on the trip, simply because he had just broken up from a five-year relationship. At only twenty years old, he felt that those five years, a quarter of his life, had been wasted. He now wanted to go on a piss-up and do some heavy drinking. He didn't care what we saw, or where we went, as long as we went drinking. His desire for adventure nearly killed us. We drank every night for five weeks. When I say every night, I don't mean one or two pints. It was at least five pints every night and often much more.

It's ironic because neither of us drinks now. I suppose that came from life learning.

My boy was here to blow off steam and sow his wild oats. However, something rather amusing happened.

My friend was too Irish.

Yes, I said it: too Irish.

My friend went to an agricultural college, rather than a mainstream University. His main areas of competence were: farming, GAA and horses. With horses, he was a prodigy. He could break horses and train them to a high level. He was skilled at buying an undervalued horse, and had the social network to sell it quickly for a higher price.

He still does this today.

He was the youngest person on that trip and the wealthiest by far. However, he struggled to talk to strangers for the first few weeks. The average person didn't know much about farming or horses, and if you're not from Ireland, you've probably never heard about the GAA.

So, he struggled to chat to people.

My friend and I tried to help him. We basically prepared a template script for him: what to say and how to chit-chat.

I learned that we can all be knowledgeable about certain areas in life, but that doesn't mean we're experts in life.

Even if you're a top lawyer or company CEO with superior knowledge in one area, that is only one area. That does not make you a knowledgeable person in general.

It's important to identify where you're knowledgeable and where you're not.

> *"The wise man is one who knows, what he does not know."*
>
> *— Lao Tzu, Tao Te Ching*

Identify what you're good at, learn where you're lacking and try to tackle it as best you can.

We also learned on that trip that false expectations can lead to anger. We went to a thermal bath party in Budapest, which, in our minds, was a sure-fire way to meet women. It was supposed to be one of the highlights of our trip. We had heard that it was like a rave, with lots of young single women, but in a thermal bath atmosphere.

Instead, it was one of the biggest sausage fests we'd ever seen. There must have been five males to every female. In preparation for lounging around in our speedos, we had spent weeks working out in the gym, but it was so dark, you couldn't see a thing. It was a waste of all our hard work.

It was also very overpriced. We started to become more and more frustrated. Our expectations were drastically not being met.

Eventually, this frustration turned to anger. This is known as the 'Frustration-Aggression Theory' (Dollard, et al 1939).

My other friend became so overwhelmed with anger combined with a large amount of alcohol that he put his fist through the window. This resulted in a massive cut close to the veins on his wrist.

When I came across his injury, he was holding his wrist and trying to wash it off in the pool. The blood didn't wash off. Instead, it started to pollute the pool, growing bigger and bigger, as though someone had been mortally wounded. It was like a scene out of the movie 'Jaws'.

We took him to the First Aider, who called an ambulance and advised he'd need stitches in hospital.

Meanwhile, conscious that the broken window was from a building that was several hundred years old, we were uncertain how much we would be charged. Drunk, and wanting to avoid fines, we decided to make a run for it.

There were two bouncers beside the ambulance. After a count of three, we sprinted past the bouncers.

My friend with the wounded hand was their main target; him and I whizzed past the bouncers. Our friend (nicknamed the "Chunky lad" of our group) wasn't as fast as us and lagged behind.

He was mauled by the two bouncers and forced to pay for a window he didn't even break.

My friend and I were chased by the bouncers in a massive park. After losing two tired bouncers when I mounted a high wall (and scraped my leg in the process), I spent hours searching for my mate. It turns out, he had hidden in a bush and fell asleep.

Although this has become one of my funny stories about my wild youth, it also taught me valuable lessons. We all have expectations, whether conscious or not, about how things are supposed to go. Whether that's about our life, jobs, relationships or friendships, we have an expectation of how they should be. If your expectations are subconscious, they're probably formed from the people around you; your parents and friends. You will most likely expect your job and life to be similar to that of your friends and family.

When an expectation is not met, it leads to frustration, and eventually to anger. This can be witnessed from certain people where their life didn't work out for them the way they wanted. Perhaps there was a divorce, a failed business or children that didn't live up to their expectations. These people never expected failure; they didn't expect to struggle after the age of thirty. The hard work was supposed to have been completed by then and everything was supposed to run smoothly after that.

Would this be your way of thinking? Or perhaps it was your thinking in the past?

Life is a struggle.

It will continue to be a struggle until the day you die.

Life is also wonderful, amazing and full of excitement. It will also be those things until the day you die.

It simply depends on whether you embrace it.

To prevent becoming angry and frustrated at life, look at your expectations. Be really honest with yourself.

Do you believe there will be a time of drastic change, when things will become easy? Do you think you'll reach a stage when you'll never become stressed or challenged?

If so, it's time to change your expectations.

Life will continue to be the same as it is now. The tasks will change and the job may change, but there will always be struggle. The only aspect that may change is your ability to cope with them. That is the only real focus; to improve your perspective and coping skills. In order to avoid months (and maybe even years) of anger, it's important to change your focus.

Identify your expectations of your life, job, relationship and friendships.

Then, **C.I.A.** them:

- What can you **C**ontrol?
- What can you **I**nfluence?
- What must you **A**ccept?

Let's look at this example: "I will have a loving wife."

What you can control:

You can control the type of person you marry and what morals they have.

What you can influence:

You can influence this by being the type of person who mirrors those values. You can have friends that are of similar morals and socioeconomic status.

What you must accept:

You must accept that people change over time. The woman you are married to at the age of forty-five is not the same woman you married when you were both twenty-five. Major life events may have happened which will have caused this change; events that are out of your control such as illness, accidents or traumatic events (e.g. the loss of a child).

To remedy this, when you notice that an expectation is causing you frustration and anger, you must change your expectations. This sounds so simple, yet the difficulty lies in recognising why you're angry and realising that it's caused by an unmet expectation.

In my experience, I have noticed that I become extremely restless and irritable when I'm stuck in a queue that I didn't anticipate. Once I realise my irritability and recognise that it's due to my expectations, I can either leave the queue or accept my position and wait twenty minutes longer than I had planned. This awareness has calmed me down so many times.

Try applying this to all areas of your life.

Notice your expectations. If they are unrealistic, change them. If you're getting angry, observe what expectation you had. Change your expectation, accept it and save yourself a lot of hardship.

I have found that this is about getting perspective on a situation. We all need to have some perspective in our lives from time to time: to be able to step back, notice what is driving our behaviour and change the way we view things. This prevents our expectations from having a negative impact on our thoughts and behaviours.

Eastern Europe trip

The following year, I went travelling through eastern Europe with my partner and love of my life.

Yet again, I learned a lot from travelling.

I had met my girlfriend when I was travelling through Europe the year before. We ended up being in the same countries at the same time. I met her on a walking tour in Vienna. I then met her again in Bratislava on what can only be described as the longest walking tour in the world.

After the walking tour, we went for drinks; me, her and our friends. It turned into a wild night. We got drunk on litre beers, then had to run for half a mile to catch our bus on time. The combination of alcohol and exercise resulted in my friend throwing up all over me on the bus.

Despite this, I arranged to have a date (with my now wife) as we were due to be in Krakow at the same time.

I would say the rest was history, but there was more to it than that.

We fell hard for each other. We were texting for over six months before I went to England to visit her.

We then started dating, with two years of our relationship being long distance. At times we didn't see each other for a month or 6 weeks due to limited finances. She was studying for a Master's degree and I had just finished mine. This, combined with the fact that my girlfriend often worked weekends, made meeting up extremely difficult.

At one stage, I remember spending a quarter of my monthly wages to see her. This was quite a struggle, but planning our eastern Europe trip felt like a reward for all our struggles. We were finally going to be together for two weeks, doing what we love.

The trip revitalised me and it revitalised our relationship. It reminded us of what we were struggling for: to be together.

The suffering failed to be suffering, when we were reminded of its meaning.

I learned that suffering pays off and that nothing lasts forever, not even the bad times.

Sometimes, all you need is some time to give perspective. You will then be revitalised and ready to continue your struggle.

I had to wait another year before we finally lived in the same country together. However, that trip was a valuable break and a reminder of why I was suffering.

We also learned about acceptance on that trip.

Having just travelled from Estonia, Latvia and Lithuania, we were just about to enter Belarus. Because Belarus wasn't in the European Union, we needed a Visa to get in. Neither of us knew much about Belarus, except for the fact that Phoebe from 'Friends' had a boyfriend who went to Minsk in Belarus.

The only reason we were visiting was because it was the next country in line. I also find you can have a much more authentic experience in lesser-known countries.

We phoned the Consulate in London who informed us that if we flew to Belarus, we would be granted an automatic holiday Visa for approximately seven days.

It was difficult from start to finish in Minsk. Belarus is a sister country to Russia, so they have similar customs. The languages spoken are

Belarussian and Russian, with English not being commonly known. Additionally, they really do not want Westerners there.

Our trip was made more difficult due to the fact that European roaming data didn't work on our phones.

However, we were well prepared.

I had printed Google maps and addresses we needed. My girlfriend could adopt the perfect 'Damsel in distress' look and people tried to help us, despite the language barrier. We also considered ourselves to be semi-experienced travellers by this point, so we were confident.

We got to the address of our hostel, but it looked like a residential apartment building. There was no sign and no indication that it was a hostel. We couldn't use our phones as we didn't have any data. It was 9pm.

For an hour we tried to find our hostel. Eventually, at 10pm, we phoned the hostel (at an extortionate foreign rate) who informed us that the buzzer was broken. They had forgotten to tell us. Also, they didn't have a sign up because it's a communist state and their business had no right to advertise over other residences.

The member of staff at the hostel also mentioned that she was just about to close the check-in desk. However, thankfully, she was going to wait for our arrival.

We honestly thought we were going to end up homeless for the night, but thankfully, we got there, checked in and slept like logs.

After having a couple of good days in Minsk, we planned to take an overnight bus to Ukraine. We arrived at the bus station early and bought our tickets. It was the only bus company that didn't assign seats when you got your ticket.

Despite being half an hour early, we headed off to buy food for the trip and use the bathroom.

Returning ten minutes before departure, we discovered that the bus driver had let people on the bus, yet no one was actually on the bus. The other passengers had got on the bus and reserved their seats by placing their bags there. All the window seats had been reserved.

I wasn't too bothered as I had my neck pillow with me. Ever since the time I hurt my neck on an overnight bus from Toronto to Quebec City, I've always come prepared with my neck pillow.

I was a bit bummed that I couldn't sit beside my girlfriend, but we were across the aisle from each other so it was fine.

The journey was actually hilarious. Some of the other passengers were drinking vodka and eating a picnic. There were others playing loud Russian gangster music.

Two old women were having a massive argument. One had reclined her seat so far back that she was practically lying on the other lady's lap. The other lady then started to push her chair repeatedly, kneeing the first lady in the back. I have no idea what they were saying, but it had to be broken up by another passenger before it got physical.

Thankfully, after an hour or so, it all quietened down and most people fell asleep.

My girlfriend suffers from travel sickness. She can tolerate a bus journey for about two hours, but after that, she starts to feel sick. She can't tolerate boat crossings at all.

We both took a sleeping tablet to help us get over the seven-hour bus journey. However, we forgot there was a border check midway.

Usually, a border check is straightforward. They come on the bus, check your passport and ask why you're travelling.

However, because we were entering Ukraine from Belarus, a country outside the European Union, we had to get off the bus at border control and go into an office.

Drowsy and half-sedated by sleeping pills, we got off the bus. Waiting our turn, we arrived in front of the border control officer.

It was very difficult as they didn't speak English. Setting my girlfriend and me to one side, they let everyone else through.

They tried communicating with us but it was a one-word conversation: "Visa".

We showed our Visa to enter Belarus.

Half an hour later, a very angry bus driver was shouting at the guards, presumably telling them we were going to be late.

Finally, an officer came on shift who could speak some basic English.

"Visa fly in, Visa fly out," he said.

Despite the fact we had phoned the Belarusian embassy twice to clarify the requirements of how to get a visa to get into the country, no-one bothered to mention a few important details. If your Visa was received by fly-in, you would have to fly out in order to leave the country.

This was despite the fact that we were both from countries that were in the European Union. Ukraine was in the European Union and we had been able to travel freely to any country in the European Union.

Pointing to my girlfriend and to myself, I said: "Europe… Ukraine, Europe, no Visa".

"Yes," he laughed.

After a few minutes of broken conversation, I gathered that we wouldn't be allowed to cross the border without the appropriate Visa.

He herded my girlfriend and me onto a bus that was going back to Minsk.

"Fly," he said.

If this situation had occurred a few years before-hand, my nerves would've been wrecked.

I would have freaked out, realising that the timeline for my trip was ruined. We were going to lose a day in Ukraine, which was a bummer because we missed out on the chance to do the Chernobyl tour.

In the past, this would have frustrated me no end. The change to our schedule was never part of my expectations and I would have struggled to gain perspective on the situation.

However, having previously thought I'd be homeless for a night in Minsk, this new situation wasn't quite as scary. I wasn't going to waste time being upset, rather, I was going to accept the situation.

I remembered the Dalai Lama's quote:

> "If a problem is fixable, if a situation is such that you can do something about it, then there is no need to worry. If it's not fixable, then there is no help in worrying. There is no benefit in worrying whatsoever."

There was nothing I could do about it, so why worry?

Our luggage was transferred from one bus to another. We were able to sit together this time. With our heavy sleeping pills, we slept like a log. I probably had one of the best night's sleep of my life.

We arrived in Minsk and booked a flight to Ukraine later that day. We waited for two hours, then got a bus to the airport and a flight to Ukraine.

This situation, which could have been a major catastrophe, ended up being a minor blip. I even have positive memories of the situation. The story is a funny tale to tell and reminds me that being adaptable and having acceptance is the best path.

If you can do something to influence or change a situation, then do. However, if you truly can't, then don't. Worrying won't add anything to the situation, except make you feel uncomfortable.

I focused on what was the best way to react. I also maximised the next thing I could control, which was enjoying the remainder of the time I had in Kyiv.

Control what you can, influence what you can and accept what you can neither control nor influence.

Southern Europe

The following year, we decided to go on a trip through southern Europe. This time, wanting to have a beach holiday, we decided to go to Croatia, Bosnia, Herzegovina and Montenegro. My friends and family were very worried about us going to Bosnia. They believed it was dangerous as they remembered the Yugoslav war at the start of the noughties. I advised them that the war was long over. Besides, I'm very close with my Grandmother, who has been to Medjugorje nearly ten times. I wanted to be able to share that experience with her.

Medjugorje is a Christian pilgrimage site in Bosnia. It wasn't my main destination in Bosnia, but, wanting to be able to talk about it with my grandmother, I spent a day there.

My grandmother knows I'm not religious but I think she was proud of me for going, even if only for her sake. This taught me the lesson that when you do something for a person that you love, it shows that you want to help and understand them. Doing something for someone else, despite your own beliefs, is appreciated by your loved ones on a much deeper level.

We embarked on our trip: in Zadar and Split, we saw the beautiful beaches of Croatia. In Bosnia, we went to Medjugorje, then on to Mostar. On a walking tour of Mostar, they told us all about the history of Bosnia; its dictatorship and the rise and fall of Yugoslavia.

It was the first time I had ever heard someone talk about a dictatorship in a positive manner. To be fair, the speaker had some valid economic and financial points as to why the country was better under a dictatorship.

We looked at the dilapidated buildings from the civil war and even climbed on one (even though I know we shouldn't have).

We spent three days in Mostar and honestly, I felt so safe the entire time; both on the Bosnian Muslim side and on the Croatian catholic side. The people were friendly, the food was good and everything was so cheap. I even contemplated getting a holiday home there. In fact, I still am.

When I told people I was going to Bosnia and eastern Europe, I had to listen to so much negative hype, but it was nothing like their misconceptions. Deep down, I was already aware of this. People judge via stereotypes, rather than making their own judgements. It's common for the human brain to do this. Stereotyping helps to stop the brain from overloading. It is tiresome having to analyse and investigate every situation. The brain files away stereotypes; mini-scripts about people, places and experiences. This saves the brain a lot of time and energy. However, there are negative side-effects from this stereotyping; preconceived dislike of people or places, without really knowing anything about them. It can even cause racism and hatred; all because of a negative stereotype.

I learned to be my own "myth buster" (or my own "stereotype buster"). I try not to believe something or presume it is common knowledge without researching or making my own assessment. Whether that's a country, a race or even a celebrity. My eyes were opened when I started to apply it to everyday life.

Be your own "myth buster". Don't assume stereotypes and do your own research.

Don't be a sheep!

Trip to Amsterdam

I had a lot of annual leave to take before the end of the year, but my girlfriend didn't have any. She also didn't have the money to go on a trip in December. Deciding to put it out there to my mates' group chat, I suggested a last-minute holiday. One of my friends was up for it. We didn't have a lot of time to plan it so we decided to pick somewhere mainstream.

We decided to go to Amsterdam and Belgium. My friend would then return home to get back to work, while I would continue myself, going to Luxembourg and Munich.

I was finally going to test myself to see if I could "solo travel" for a week. It was always something I had wanted to try.

My friend and I had great fun and saw all the sights in Amsterdam. However, it was a conversation in a bar that changed both our lives.

It was one of those conversations where you ask "if there's more to life". I was miserable in my job. My boss was incompetent and I was doing half her work. I was underpaid and in the wrong field. I was starting to become someone I didn't like. All for what? Just to gain management experience and move up the ladder. Yes, I was climbing the ladder but I hadn't even checked if it was at the right building.

My friend was in a job he was good at, but he was indifferent about the work. He had tried to leave the company, attending interviews and gaining offers from other companies. However, when this happened, his current company would match their offer and he stayed where he was.

We were both twenty-five years old and dreading a lifetime stuck in the same path. We began to contemplate our careers and question what we wanted from life.

This was the first truly deep conversation during that trip, but many followed.

I wanted a new job in an area I was passionate about. I wanted to set up my own business, just as my parents had done. At the end of my working life, I wanted to be able to say: "I created that".

My friend wanted to do what he'd always wanted to do, which was to be a physio. However, he felt he couldn't leave his job due to financial reasons. We chatted about it in length and after several days, we had a plan of action to change our lives.

I bought my first rental property and began my journey of being financially independent. I also applied for, and got a job working with young people in a youth charity. I loved that job.

My friend mustered up the courage to ask his father for his grandmother's cottage which had been left idle. He has since renovated it. He now lives in a beautiful, traditional, but modern, cottage mortgage-free. He left his job, retrained as a physio and now does that full time.

Although the outcomes are great, it didn't run as smoothly as it sounds.

I learned so much from those few days. Firstly, it is brave and beneficial to be emotionally vulnerable with friends. Instead of pretending to be happy, I'm grateful I had the courage to say to my friend: "Life is sh** right now and I want something different". I realised there's strength in being vulnerable. It allows others to be vulnerable with you too and it leads to open and deep conversations which promote change.

This concept is supported by the 'Law of Reciprocity' in psychology. It's based on the premise that if you do something for someone, they feel indebted to pay it back. It doesn't just encompass practical favours; it also takes into account emotional favours. If you share personal information with someone, they're likely to feel obligated to share personal information too. On this occasion, it was successful with my friend. However, it's also a method I use when trying to communicate with hard-to-reach youths.

The second thing I learned, which I've already touched upon, is the importance of the people I spend my time with.

My friend and I were able to support and push each other to tackle our goals. The most beneficial thing we did was to make the other person believe they could achieve their goals and reach their potential. A reminder of the quote from Jim Rohn:

> *"You are the average of the five people you spend the most time with."*

Be selective about who you're hanging out with. If I didn't have a friend like him, I would still be unhappy. Imagine if he had responded with:

"Everyone's unhappy, suck it up!" Some other guy might have said: "Your goals are unachievable, let's make them realistic."

If your friends give you advice like that, get new friends. Their words would only be chains holding you back. Be selective about the people you spend your time with. You're giving them a portion of your life, whether you're aware of it or not. If they're using a portion of your life to restrict you or hold you back, then you owe it to yourself to find new friends. There's no need to have a dramatic conversation with them about it, but slowly drift away. Don't let yourself be vulnerable with these types of people. Find people who help you to believe that you can achieve your goals.

Over the years, I've had a bit of a purge of friends, but I can honestly say, it's one of the best things I've ever done.

Trip to Wales with Dad, 2021

In 2021, my father and I went on a road trip around Wales. At that time, my dad had only left Ireland once in the previous ten years. I had some annual leave to take by the end of the year. My girlfriend didn't have any annual leave left as she had been to England to visit her family. We were in the process of looking for a house to buy so I wanted a cheap holiday and didn't want to go too far afield.

I mentioned to my dad that I was going on a trip with my friend Jack. My father loves Jack as they're both interested in farming. Dad seemed really interested in the trip, so I asked him if he wanted to come along.

I was expecting a firm "no", but he mulled it over for a few days. Eventually, with a bit of arm twisting, he decided to come. Mam wasn't too happy about it—he hadn't been on a holiday with her for years!

In the end, Jack injured his leg in a soccer match and decided not to come on the trip. After all, there would be quite a bit of walking.

Dad and I travelled the length and breadth of Wales for a week. A lot of time was spent in the car driving, which was a great opportunity for us to talk and catch up. I feel like we talked about our whole lives during those few days.

We talked about other family members and their successes. We talked about the past; both mine and my siblings. We talked about our childhood and teenage years; all the pros and cons, as well as the good memories. We talked about how you view life differently, depending on your age.

Dad reflected on his own past; how he felt that he had probably worked too much and held on to money for the next work project. He owned a farm, while my mother was a horse-riding instructor. Together, they built a business consisting of the biggest indoor horse-riding centre in southern Ireland. It had sixty stables, a horse walker, a small cross country and two large outdoor arenas. This, combined with other investments spanning thirty years, was very impressive to me.

However, it wasn't an easy journey for them. It's a huge commitment when you have to feed sixty horses every day—whether that's Christmas day, your birthday or before a Sunday family outing. The business was 'touch and go' for a few years at the start, but eventually, it became a success.

The success was down to the fact that my father reinvested the money back into the business, expanding and diversifying. I now view this as a great accomplishment, although in hindsight, as a teenager, I would have been more impressed if the money was pumped into a fancier car, designer clothes or foreign holidays. However, I learned from their example.

Why would my father have regret? He regrets delaying his happiness.

"I'll be happy when I have another ten stables."

"I'll be happy when I expand the outdoor arena for dressage shows."

"I'll be happy when I get a horse walker."

The regret was not in wanting those things, but in waiting for them to make him happy.

Material items can't make you happy. Well, they can for a short time, but the law of familiarity means that the happiness fades very quickly.

We're all guilty of waiting for life to improve. We tend to live in the future rather than living right now in the present moment.

Most of us are guilty of valuing money rather than valuing time spent with our loved ones.

There were a few things that Dad mentioned which showed he hadn't come to terms with some of his decisions. From this, I learned that:

"When thinking about life, no amount of guilt can change the past and no amount of anxiety can change the future"

– Unknown

We all try to do our best, but inevitably, we all make mistakes and have regrets. Having regrets in life isn't always a bad thing. It simply means that you had important decisions to make in life

283

and those decisions were important enough to get wrong.

There are people in life who won't make their own decisions. They rely on parents or close friends to make their decisions for them. If it's a wrong decision, they blame the person that gave the advice. They take no accountability for their own choices.

Don't be afraid to make a decision. At the very least, you will learn from it.

- If you're in the wrong career, take action and move into the area of work that you're passionate about.
- If you're working too much, look at your schedule and cut something out.
- If you're not happy, try to find a purpose in your life.
- If you can change it, then do. If you can't, then don't worry about it.

Most people don't like to apologise because it makes them feel vulnerable. People convince themselves that the person they have wronged knows they regret it, so they don't need to apologise. That is a lie.

A simple apology goes a long way. "I was wrong. This is why I made my decision. I'm sorry."

My father apologised to me about many different things. Most of which he was not at fault for.

If you can't change the past and you have already apologised, then forget about it. Otherwise, all you're doing is beating yourself up over something you can't control. It's pointless suffering. Release yourself from this prison of regret and allow yourself to be forgiven.

It was once said to me: "Stop whipping yourself and forgive."

It set me free, so I say the same to you: "Stop whipping yourself and forgive."

As a youth worker, I said the same thing to numerous parents and it made a huge difference for them.

If you have any regret, especially with a loved one:

- change it if you can,
- apologise if you can't
- forgive yourself.

Another major lesson I learned on this trip was that it was a privilege to spend time with my father. One week by ourselves with no interruptions.

It was great to have lengthy periods of leisure time together to delve into deeper conversations, rather than our usual, day-to-day, surface level chat about work, mortgages and current affairs. Instead, we have time to reflect on the past and gain perspective on each other's lives. We could share wisdom and knowledge, as both student and teacher to each other.

I never imagined I would have a travelling experience with my dad. He is a man who normally lives and works within a five-mile radius of his house. I am so grateful to cherish those memories with him. I'm also grateful that I seized the opportunity to whisk him away for once!

The lesson for me was: take advantage of the time you have with your family and loved ones. It is for this reason that, when tackling the 'destination' side of my bucket list, I always try to go with family or friends.

Of course, if family or friends are unable to travel, then I would still encourage solo-travel because it's such a great experience.

However, if you want more time with your parents or loved ones, before it's too late, then I would definitely invite them. It becomes so routine to go on holiday with our partner. We don't even think about going with parents, siblings or friends. Some of you might say: "That's because they drive me crazy!" However, if you value their relationship, then one holiday in a lifetime isn't too much to sacrifice. Try to plan a holiday with family members as part of your bucket list, or at least the family members who have a positive influence on your life!

Running with the Bulls in Pamplona 2023

In July 2023, I took on one of the most daunting tasks of my bucket list: Running with the Bulls in Pamplona. Bull running occurs all over Spain, but Pamplona is the biggest and best-known location.

I have wanted to run with bulls ever since I was a teenager. I suppose I secretly wanted to have a "hard man persona". To me, running with the bulls was such a daredevil thing to do, warranting respect and admiration from others, all of which were important goals to me as a teen.

Years later, as an adult in my late twenties, I still wanted to do it, but my motivation had changed. I was no longer seeking the hard man persona. That didn't interest me anymore. However, I wanted to do it because it scared me. I wanted to conquer a monumental fearful challenge so that I could refer to it as a metaphorical signpost in the future. If I became nervous about delivering training to new staff at work, I could say to myself:

> *"Come on man, you ran with the bulls in Pamplona, you can do this!"*

It would act as a reminder of the courage and confidence I had, in order to perform the task ahead.

Best friend by my side, I set off to run with the bulls. My friend was there as my support and observer. He joked he was there to identify my body.

We arrived in Pamplona late at night, around 10.30pm, and then proceeded to stay out until 3am, enjoying the festivities. That evening, I tried to walk along the route of the bull run to get a scope of the day ahead. However, the route was along city streets which were full of people drinking, singing and enjoying the San Fermin festival. It was impossible to gain a true reflection of the course.

I never did find out where it started. However, based on the videos I had watched, I chose a spot. It was approximately 10 metres from "Dead man's corner".

Yes, that's right: "Dead man's corner".

There's a point in the course where the bulls run down a hill and take a sharp right hand turn at the bottom. They nearly always crash into the left-hand side of the street. It has a metal door which blocks off one of the streets and directs the bulls to the street leading to the stadium.

I chose a spot after this point. The bulls would have either slowed down or crashed into the side, reducing their speed. As the bulls crash on the left hand side, they tend to group together after the corner, which makes that side of the street very dangerous. You can't get away from them.

To be honest, I got freaked out about it. Realistically, although called "Dead Man's Corner", very few people have died from running with bulls. The last reported death from the event was in 2009, however there have been a lot of injuries. According to the statistics, the reported injuries were only of a minor nature. Minor injuries reported were cuts or bruises from tripping over other people, rather than injuries from the bulls.

Of course, there are people who have been badly injured, but considering there are approximately 1700-2000 people at each event, it's highly unlikely that I would be the one to be gored by a bull.

I remember my friend telling me that I didn't have to do it; that I could back out. He would tell people that I did do it; no-one would be any the wiser. That was very kind of him, but I knew that wasn't me. I couldn't pretend to do something and lie to everyone about it. I'm just not that kind of person.

I decided to go ahead and do it, but I learned a valuable lesson. I learned that it doesn't matter how many crazy things you do or how many times you try to conquer fear, the fear will always be there. It was something I had to accept. However, I knew I was going to do it, despite the fear. That is the type of person I want to be and that's the type of person a lot of people aspire to be.

So, the next day, I did it. My plan worked. The bulls took a hard left around the bend. I got close enough to them while still having space on my right to escape when I needed to.

I noticed some other people; in particular, one man in a purple t-shirt. He was parallel to me on the left-hand side. The first three bulls hit the dead man's corner. They congregated on the left-hand side of the street; three bulls wide. The man in purple was trapped, people to his right and three bulls behind him. He had nowhere to go.

He was hit from behind by the fastest bull and launched into the air. The poor chap landed on the ground and was trampled by the other two bulls. He had to be rushed to hospital with an expected brain injury. However, I found out later that thankfully he was fine and had made a great recovery.

This reiterated the lesson:

"If you fail to prepare, prepare to fail."

We have touched upon acceptance earlier and we have talked about suffering. Both of which applied to the man in the purple shirt. He had to:

- suffer the injury and accept he made a poor decision
- or accept he didn't prepare for the dangerous task he embarked upon.

Either way, he must take accountability and move on.

This is a lesson that we can all apply when suffering comes our way. I learned a lot from that man, despite having never actually met him.

By now, you may be thinking,

"Yes Shane, I get it—when travelling, you can learn important life lessons and you can try to be the best person you can be. You can push yourself outside of your comfort zone. However, you can also do this during everyday life!"

I agree one hundred percent. You don't need to travel in order to learn valuable life lessons or to strive to be the best you can be. In fact, being the best person you can be is often maximised by repetition and routine. You should learn from everyday experiences and try to better yourself every day.

However, it's innate human nature to seek pleasure and avoid pain.

Due to this, most people overindulge in pleasure as a result of their base animalistic desires: eating too much food, bingeing on TV, and watching porn. They avoid pain as much as possible; putting off going to the gym, delaying tough conversations with family and procrastinating on inward self-reflection.

However, this doesn't promote growth or personal development. It helps sometimes if people are removed from their daily environment and daily routine in order to challenge themselves.

They return with a heightened sense of accomplishment which aids them in implementing (and maintaining) their progress in their day-to-day lives. In addition, the lessons they have learned are remembered with more clarity because they're associated positively with a holiday or vacation.

We often forget we learned something when it occurred during our monotonous day-to-day life, but we clearly remember lessons from events we enjoyed. Studies have shown that events holding emotional significance are more likely to be remembered vividly than mundane experiences (McGaugh, 2004).

When we're on holiday, we're usually happier. Holidays are rare as they generally only happen twice a year. Learning from a holiday is easier to remember as it's more prominent in our mind.

Use your holidays, not only to see sights, but to venture out of your comfort zone and tackle your shortcomings. By using holidays in this way, you will maximise your development and have a greater chance of implementing the lessons into your everyday life.

The Camino (The French Way) 2023

The Camino de Santiago is a world-renowned pilgrimage of mediaeval origin. Pilgrims journey to the Cathedral of Santiago de Compostela in the northwest of Spain. It is believed that the remains of the Apostle St. James the Great were buried in the Cathedral. However, according to some historians, this was a pilgrimage site long before Christianity. Celts and Pagans left Spain (and neighbouring countries) to travel to the north of the country in order to reach the "End of the

World"; a place called 'Finisterre'. Finisterre was the most western point of Spain. It was believed to be the end of the world prior to the discovery of Ireland, Britain, and then the Americas. The sun also set in the West which made Celts and Romans believe that the sun slept at the end of the world, past Finisterre.

Finisterre is roughly 90 kilometres outside Santiago. In Finisterre, there is an old camp with houses built of stone by the Celts. There are many dolmens all along the road. Historians believed that people looked at the sky and used the stars to navigate their way to Finisterre. Some believe this is why the region is called 'Santiago de Compostela', with 'Compestela' translating to 'the field of stars'.

The Christian Church has taken up this tradition of pilgrimage and claims that Saint James' body lies in Santiago. St. James died in Palestine in 44AD. In my opinion, it's quite unlikely that his body came to Spain, even after his death. However, after doing your own research, you may come to your own decision. I'm just giving a small bit of background. It's also important to highlight that visiting a pilgrimage doesn't necessarily have to be for religious reasons. I chose to visit for my own personal development.

I completed it the French way. On this route, you start in France, at 'Saint-Jean-Pied-de-Port', walk over the Pyrenees mountains, through northern Spain and into Santiago de Compostela. The route is approximately 780 kilometres and can take anywhere from 28 to 35 days, depending on your speed. Due to the length of this trip, it isn't one of those experiences that will "just happen"—you have to prepare for this trip financially, physically and mentally.

I had three weeks to journey as much as I could, before returning to work. Due to limitations on time, I had to skip the 'Meseta', which is the desert section in the middle. The designated, suggested amount of walking was approximately 20km per day. I walked 30km every day for nineteen days. In total, I walked 564km. It wasn't the full amount, but it was still a lot. Many of the other pilgrims were in their mid-to-late fifties with no constraints on their time or schedule. Some pilgrims were in their twenties. Very few were in the thirties and forties range. I would imagine this was due to having dependent children.

I was 29 years old at the time. I'm so glad I took the time out to do it when I did. If I didn't do it then, I could be in my mid-fifties before I got the chance to do it.

I've learned that it's better to do something NOW and make the most of the experience while you can, instead of holding off. If I held off on the experience, waiting for the right time to do the full circuit (and not miss out on the 'Meseta' section), the time might never have come.

I missed out on 220 km which would've taken 8 days. I know I could have done it and I would have done it. However, financially, I had to get back to work to save money for other trips, such as my best friend's wedding.

Most pilgrims fly into Santiago, get a bus and walk the last 100 km. They still get their Certificate of Completion. So, I did more than most and I'm so happy I did it.

I learned to do things NOW; to make the most of the present. You never know what's down the line.

> *"Do not do something tomorrow that you can do today."*
>
> *– Old Proverb*

The Camino was my best teacher for learning how to stay in the present moment. I was always reflecting on the past and planning for the future. I would look at the past and say:

"I liked that—I want that in my life again."

Or: "I didn't like that so I don't want that in my life again."

Then I would plan for my future:

"I'll go here on holidays. I'll try to invest in this. I'll do this."

Reflecting on the past and planning for the future are great skills which everyone should do. However, I was overdoing it. I needed to stay in the present moment. I was always living in the future; planning and scheming. I had drawn up my:

- 1 year plan
- 5-year plan
- 10-year plan

The Camino gave me time to reflect on the past and plan for the future. However, I realised that I had exhausted my plans about the future.

I was planning for scenarios that might never happen at all. It was okay planning for likely scenarios but planning for every single eventuality was time-consuming and, in a sense, wasteful. I had a 10-year plan. Initially, I reflected on the past a lot. At first, it was mostly negative, but later I focused on the positives. Reflecting on the past helped me to learn. The contrast between positivity versus negativity gave me the comfort that I had more good experiences than bad. It takes time to reflect, but the Camino gave me the ability to do that.

After five days on Camino, I had spent a lot of time planning and reflecting. Then the pain of the blisters kicked in. Weirdly, the pain centred me. Walking with the pain of several blisters meant that my mind wouldn't let me focus anywhere else but on the here and now. To distract myself, I chatted with other pilgrims and focused on the beautiful scenery around me. Even when the pain left me after a few days, the habit of staying in the here and now, remained. For once in my life, I was truly in the moment; walking, eating, chatting and observing the beauty around me. Just being present. It was an amazing lesson.

Another lesson the Camino taught me was to listen. I met people from literally all over the world. If we walked together long enough, we would have (what I would call) a "Camino conversation". This is when two strangers have a deep, meaningful conversation and share inti-mate details about their life. There is no fear of repercussions because, the chances are, you're unlikely to see that person ever again. They don't know any of your friends or associates.

I chatted with people who struggled with various issues such as self-harm, suicide attempts, infertility and relationship break-ups. Several people talked about their divorce, especially people in their fifties whose marriage had broken down when their children left home.

It taught me the power of healing, just from being listened to. It taught me that I don't have to try to solve problems for people. In fact, they don't want you to. More often than not, people just want to feel listened to. I truly learned the power of active listening; which is listening to understand rather than respond.

I'm so grateful to those people who shared their stories with me. Because I didn't know their background, their full situation, family, culture or even their first language, I couldn't offer advice. The problem-solver in me struggled! However, I learned that not every problem needs to be solved. More often than not, emotional problems need to be felt and understood. That's what I tried to do.

It also helped to reinforce the mindset of gratitude. We have no idea what other people are going through. An old man once said to me:

> "If everyone put their problems on a table together, you would be very quick to pick your own back up again."

When you observe other people's battles, your own problems don't seem as bad in comparison. Hearing about other people's struggles helps you to realise that your own problems are manageable. Another valuable lesson I gained from my time on the Camino is that:

You don't need much to be happy.

Most people who embark on the Camino pack too much, then realise that, because they have to carry everything on their back, they need to leave things behind or post them back home.

You need very little on the Camino.

I had 3 T-shirts, 3 pairs of shorts, 3 pairs of socks, underwear, a pair of walking shoes and flip flops, a toiletry bag, towel, sleeping bag and charger. That's it.

I didn't need anything else. It was a lesson in minimalism: you don't need material stuff to be happy. The best things in life are experiences and positive human interaction, both of which can be done cheaply.

When I look back at my time on the Camino, I remember the scenery, the people I chatted with, the feeling of contentment and being in the present moment. I don't remember what I was eating or what I was wearing. It was nice to come home to decent meals and a full wardrobe, but I remembered how easily I lived without them. I think it took away the fear of what will happen if I lose everything. It would be difficult, but I know I would survive. I would even have as much a chance of being happy as I do now.

The Camino taught me so many lessons. If you want to read more about the Camino, there are so many books about it. For me, these were the major lessons that I think everyone learns when they are a pilgrim.

After these main lessons, I believe everyone will learn something different, depending on what stage of life they're at.

The saying goes: "The Camino provides."

The Camino has always been on my bucket list, ever since I watched "The Way" in religion class at the age of sixteen.

Due to writing my bucket list and being intentional with my time, I finally accomplished it, twelve and a half years later.

It wasn't easy. I had to leave my comfort zone. I had to travel to France by myself, walking for hours on my own. However, what I gained from it was substantial.

It's important to set goals on your bucket list, even if you don't think you can complete it immediately. You won't be the same person in twelve years' time. Your future self may be able to complete the task you once believed was impossible.

CHAPTER TWELVE

Bucket list sights: Quality or Quantity approach?

I HAVE SPOKEN AT LENGTH about the intrinsic value of a bucket list. I have talked about how it's not just about seeing sights, but a means towards personal development and self-actualisation. However, you do need to identify which sights you wish to see, in order to plan your trips and give you a sense of direction and accomplishment.

Let's discuss two strategies for selecting sights and destinations.

Quality

Writing your travel destination list can be done in two ways: Quality or Quantity.

Both styles require you to research. You should buy a few travel books. Look up sights and countries that you've never heard of. You won't know what you want if you don't know what's out there. Educate yourself. Spend several days or weeks reading blogs and travel books to discover which places you'd like to see.

However, beware of *'paralysis by analysis'*. You won't know if you like a country or a sight until you go there. Don't be afraid to factor in a location in case you might not like it. Perhaps it doesn't live up to your expectations, but that's part and parcel of the adventure of travelling.

Some of my favourite sights (and experiences) were in lesser-known places, such as:

- "The Hill of Crosses" in Lithuania
- The city of Rega in Latvia
- Jumping off the bridge in Mostar (Bosnia and Herzegovina)

It takes time and research, but it's a life-changing task, so take your time. However, it is important to eventually finish writing your bucket list. You'll only hinder yourself if you keep putting it off.

Once you've researched various countries and sites around the world, you could begin with the 'Quality' approach. The quality approach focuses on narrowing a list of 30 or 40 destinations down to 10 and then halving them to 5. This is done for many reasons. Firstly, if you have too many destinations, it can feel too overwhelming.

Completion may seem unachievable, therefore you may never start.

Having five destinations makes the goal seem achievable. It aids people who are hesitant about the challenge. Most people have only a few places they want to see. However, many people become side-tracked by wanting to travel to other places, just to keep up with the Joneses. Having simply five destinations will keep you focused.

The 'Quality' approach works well for middle-aged and mature adults. People within this age bracket are likely to have more money, but less time. They can afford to go on five trips within the next 5-10 years.

When you narrow your list down to five dream destinations, you're more likely to see one destination during one trip. For example, let's say you want to see the Sydney opera house and you also want to see Santorini in Greece. These two destinations will most likely take place over two separate trips. One is in Australia and the other is in Europe; the other side of the world.

When applying the 'Quality' approach, you may only be able to embark on one destination. The two sights you want to see may be too far from each other, making it difficult to accomplish in one trip. This is achievable due to the fact that you have fewer destinations to see.

If you're a bit older and more financially stable, but with less time on your hands, then I would suggest taking the 'Quality' approach. If you manage to complete your five dream destinations, then I would suggest focusing on remaining tasks on your bucket list. Perhaps you could travel to destinations that will help you to conquer those tasks.

For example, if you want to conquer your fear of heights, you could go to Slovenia and skydive near Lake Bled. Alternatively, you could go to Colorado in the US and try rock climbing.

Your target for completing the tasks is to improve your self-development, rather than just travel destinations. This is a great approach for someone who is just embarking upon a bucket list or for someone who thinks they're too old to start.

Choose your top ten sights in the world, halve them to just five and get started!

Quantity

The second approach to selecting travel sights for your bucket list is the 'Quantity' approach. This approach focuses on the number of destinations you want to visit. Whilst striving for a lot of destinations, I would advise you to keep a note of your desired top three ultimate sights. I would then set a goal of the number of sights you wish to see.

For example:

- 20 of the best sights in America
- 3 top sights whilst travelling through Europe, Asia or Africa.

This was the approach I used. The best way to do this was by looking through a 'Lonely Planet' travel book, which shows the top 500 places to see in the world.

My goal was to see 50 places out of the top 500.

I would then be able to say that I had visited one-tenth of the top places in the world.

When one of my friends suggested going somewhere or if I found myself visiting a country I hadn't intended to, I opened the travel book and located nearby 'top places' in the area. I would then be able to visit them and check them off my list.

This approach also helped me when I was planning trips through mid, south and eastern Europe. Travelling through Europe by train was great as it allowed me to see the most sights in the least amount of time. It was also relatively cheap.

This 'Quantity' approach gave me intentionality. It suited me because I was young and had more free time. Additionally, there are so many sights in Europe making it easier to reach my goal.

By the time I was 25 years old, and in the space of 5 years, I had seen 50 of the top sights in the world.

This 'Quantity' approach helped me to visit magnificent destinations, some of which I had never even heard of before. It also encouraged me to visit lesser-known countries. It showed me how to maximise my time in each country I visited.

This 'Quantity' approach is better suited to younger people who have more time than money. They may not have the money to jet to the other side of the world, but they have time during the summer to travel around their own country or neighbouring countries.

This approach encourages you to take advantage of opportunities that present themselves; for example:

- Cheap flights to a neighbouring country
- Vouchers from one hotel that you can use in their sister hotel in another country.

This 'Quantity' approach makes the most of your free time and a limited budget. I strongly suggest obtaining a travel guide or list of sights. Otherwise, you won't find the inspiration to travel to lesser-known countries.

There is no better feeling than striking a line through the name of a destination in your travel guide. It's deeply satisfying to look at all your crossed-out destinations!

Choose one of the two above approaches, depending on your circumstances, budget and time constraints.

- Write the destination (or number of destinations) on your bucket list.
- Start being intentional with your holidays.
- Start tackling the sights on your list.
- Stop dreaming about your bucket list and start living it!

As Mark Twain famously said:

"Twenty years from now you will be more disappointed by the things you didn't do than by the ones you did do. So throw off the bowlines. Sail away from the safe harbour. Catch the trade winds in your sails. Explore. Dream. Discover."

Creating your bucket list

Bucket list template:

Now that I have explained the reasoning behind each task on the list, I am going to give you a working template. If you're unsure why something has been included on the list, then please refer back to the relevant chapter for an explanation.

1. Identify the <u>wrong</u> reasons to make a bucket list. Ensure you're not doing it for those reasons.

For example:

- Is your bucket list a competition against a sibling or parent?
- Are you following a bucket list to create an illusion of yourself as successful on social media?
- Are you pursuing a bucket list to escape your life and the people in it?

Think long and hard about these points (or any other alternatives that may arise) to see if you're following a bucket list for the right reasons. If it's for the wrong reasons, unfortunately you won't be resilient enough to endure the tough times. You need to be motivated enough to emerge out of your comfort zone, challenge yourself to conquer your fears and strive to be the best you can be.

2. Choose a 'Quantity' or 'Quality' approach regarding the sights you want to see.

If you're younger than thirty, I would recommend trying the 'Quantity' approach. Try to see 50 of the top 500 places in the world. This is the stage of life where you probably have more time than money. It will (hopefully) be easier for you to take longer periods off work.

If you're above thirty, I would recommend the 'Quality' approach. Choose the top 5 sights in the world that you'd like to see. No add-ons. No distractions.

3. Self-awareness

(a) Use Maslow's 'Hierarchy of Needs' to identify your own personal needs (relative to physiological, safety, love and belonging, esteem and self-actualisation). If necessary, have conversations with your parents (or guardians) about the past. Set your own personal plan of how you will amend circumstances in the future.

(b) Look at the characteristics of a self-actualised person. Observe which qualities you need to develop. Put them on your list.

_____

_____

_____

_____

(c) Notice the ways in which you have been conditioned by society and the ways in which you would like to be unique.

_____

_____

_____

_____

(d) Have a Socratic meeting with yourself. Identify the areas in your life that you would like to change. Discover any maladaptive coping strategies you have in your life. Target the areas you want to change.

_____

_____

_____

_____

(e) Carry out a 'Value exercise'. Observe what you value in an individual.

_____

_____

_____

4. Analyse what you have discovered about yourself in the self-awareness section.

Acknowledge the changes you need to make in order to live a life that is in line with your values. Changes that will help you to meet your unmet needs.

Focus on tasks and activities. For example, if you want to learn how to trust your own judgement, it would be a good idea to try solo travel.

Maybe you have to change your job in order to become more in line with your values. There might be some tasks that you're not able to do straight away. Some tasks might scare you (such as quitting your job)! However, it's important to write them down anyway, knowing that some-day, your future self will be brave enough to do them.

_____

_____

_____

_____

_____

_____

313

5. Make a list of your fears. Write a course of action regarding how to overcome them.

For example, I was terrified of water. I took over thirty swimming lessons. I conquered my fear when I jumped from a pier into the sea.

_____

_____

_____

6. Choose the life hacks that will help you in your daily life.

Create a morning and evening routine.

Life hacks are: Mindfulness, gratitude, affirmations, basic CBT, etc.

_____

_____

_____

_____

7. Become financially stable. Implement the lessons from the financial chapter into your life. It will be very difficult to create the time to truly tackle your bucket list if you're not, in some way, financially stable.

8. "To be generous to others, you need to believe you are worthy of Love". If you already have this belief, that's great. However, think about whether you actually believe it deep down in your heart. If you do believe it, your goal should involve becoming a consistently generous person. Volunteer or give back. In some way, make the world a better place.

9. (a) Have one **holiday** with your close friends

(b) Have one **holiday** with your parents.

10. Try to find your purpose in life. This is something you want to achieve with your life, usually something that benefits others. This could take you many years to discover, but by the end of the bucket list, you'll be a lot closer to it than when you started. Who knows, you will probably discover it while you're on the journey of completing your list.

You must write your bucket list down on a piece of paper and put it somewhere visible. If the bucket list isn't written and visible, then it's not real. A bucket list is not an abstract thought. A bucket list is a tangible object that forces its owner to take accountability and responsibility for its completion. **If your bucket list is not written down, then you don't have one.**

Farewell

BY NOW, YOU HAVE READ MY PERSONAL EXPERIENCES and you have written your bucket list.

Now, take the time to think about it.

Think about it during the day and think about it in the evening.

Let your mind become consumed by it.

The more you think about your bucket list, the more your desire grows.

Napoleon Hill famously said:

"The starting point of all achievement is DE-SIRE. Keep this constantly in mind. Weak desire brings weak results, just as a small fire makes a small amount of heat."

Create your desire through consistent thoughts.

Do not 'set it and forget it'.

Spend the initial weeks (or even months) that are required to become self-aware.

See what tasks you can start off with: maybe something small, but try to start straight away. It doesn't have to be a big task, maybe just join a dancing class because you've always wanted to but were too afraid. After you learn or improve, use that newfound confidence to continue on and then tackle the next goal.

Many of us often feel too overwhelmed to tackle great goals such as a bucket list.

However, the bucket list is about doing small things consistently and in a great way.

You will make many mistakes.

You might try a task that you're not ready for yet, then stop, then come back to it later.

You might confront your parents about your childhood and it might not be a positive outcome.

Your journey will be full of ups and downs.

However, as long as you stay consistent and keep trying, you will get there. You will see the progress you have made.

To not have a bucket list is to not live life with intentionality.

To not have a bucket list is to risk not becoming the best person you can be.

By not being intentional with your time, and being less than you can be, are the ingredients for regret.

To leave you with the words of Oscar Wilde:

"Live life with no excuses, travel with no regret."

References

Bstan-'dzin-rgya-mtsho., Tutu, D., & Abrams, D. C. (2016). The book of joy: lasting happiness in a changing world. First large print edition. New York: Random House Large Print

Clason, G. S. (1955). *The richest man in Babylon*. New York: Hawthorn.

Csikszentmihalyi, M. (1997). Finding flow.

Csikszentmihalyi, M. (1975). Beyond boredom and anxiety. San Francisco, CA: Jossey-Bass.

Csikszentmihalyi, M. (1982). Toward a psychology of optimal experience. In L. Wheeler (Ed.), Review of personality and social psychology (pp. 13-36). Beverly Hills, CA: Sage.

Csikszentmihalyi, M. (1986). Lo studio dell'esperienza quotidiana [The study of everyday experience]. In F. Massimini & P. Inghilleri (Eds.), L'esperienza quotidiana (pp. 107-132). Milan, Italy: Angeli Editore.

Csikszentmihalyi, M., & Kubey, R. W. (1981). Television and the rest of life: A systematic comparison of subjective experience. Public Opinion Quarterly, 45, 317-328.

Csikszentmihalyi, M., & Larson, R. (1984). Being adolescent. New \brk: Basic Books.

Csikszentmihalyi, M., & Larson, R. (1987). Validity and reliability of the experience sampling method. Journal of Nervous and Mental Disease, 775,526-536.

Csikszentmihalyi, M., & LeFevre, J. (1989). Optimal experience in work and leisure. *Journal of personality and social psychology, 56*(5), 815.

Dixit, J. (2008, November 1s). The Art of Now: Six Steps to Living in the Moment. Retrieved February 14, 2021, from https://www. psychologytoday.com/us/articles/200811/ the-art-now-six-steps-living-in-the-moment.

Frankl, V. (1997). *Man's search for meaning*. London: Pocket Books.

Mentovich, A. and Jost, John T. (2017, August 11). *frustration-aggression hypothesis. Encyclopaedia Britannica.* https://www.britannica.com/ science/frustration-aggression-hypothesis.

Murphy, M. A. (2017). *Hiring for attitude: A revolutionary approach to recruiting star performers with both tremendous skills and superb attitude*. New York: McGraw-Hill Education.

Bstan-'dzin-rgya-mtsho., Tutu, D., Abrams, D. C., Chau, F., & James, P. F. (2016). *The book of joy: lasting happiness in a changing world.* Unabridged. [New York]: [Westminster, MD]: Penguin Random House.

B. (2014, April 02). About Biography. Retrieved January 17, 2021, from https://www.biography.com/page/about.

Boyd, R., & Richerson, P. J. (2009). Culture and the evolution of human cooperation. *Philosophical transactions of the Royal Society of London. Series B, Biological sciences, 364*(1533), 3281–3288. https://doi.org/10.1098/rstb.2009.0134.

Emerson, Ralph Waldo, 1803-1882. (1967). Self-reliance. White Plains, N.Y.: Peter Pauper Press.

Jeffrey, S. (n.d.). Ultimate list of core values. Retrieved from https://scottjeffrey.com/core-values-list/.

Kaufman, S. B. (2018, November 7). What Does It Mean to Be Self-Actualized in the 21st Century? Retrieved from https://blogs.scientificamerican.com/beautiful-minds/what-does-it-mean-to-be-self-actualized-in-the-21st-century/.

McGonigal, K. (2010, December 14). Why We Need a Little Fear. Retrieved February 08, 2020, from https://www.psychologytoday.com/us/blog/the-science-willpower/201012/why-we-need-little-fear.

Raghunathan, R. (2014, January 18). The Need to Love. Psychology Today. https://www.psychologytoday.com/us/blog/sapient-nature/201401/the-need-love.

Sternberg, R. J. (1988). The triangle of love. New York: Basic.

Tredgold, G. (2016, June 1). *49 quotes that will help you avoid the blame game.* Inc.com. https://www.inc.com/gordon-tredgold/49-quotes-that-will-help-you-avoid-the-blame-game.html.

Printed in Great Britain
by Amazon

58689234R00185